H. L. Smith

Mary and I Go to Europe

An unbiased account of a little journey in the world during the months of June, July,

and August, 1896

H. L. Smith

Mary and I Go to Europe
An unbiased account of a little journey in the world during the months of June, July, and August, 1896

ISBN/EAN: 9783337214357

Printed in Europe, USA, Canada, Australia, Japan

Cover: Foto ©Andreas Hilbeck / pixelio.de

More available books at **www.hansebooks.com**

MARY AND I
GO TO
EUROPE.

Published By
HENDRICK HUDSON CHAPTER,
DAUGHTERS OF THE AMERICAN REVOLUTION,
HUDSON, N. Y.
For the Benefit of
The Chapter Building Fund.

Mary and I Go to Europe.

AN UNBIASED ACCOUNT

(*E. & O. E.*)

OF

A LITTLE JOURNEY IN THE WORLD

DURING THE MONTHS

OF

JUNE, JULY AND AUGUST,

1896.

BY

A. PILLER, Doctor.

Published By

HENDRICK HUDSON CHAPTER, DAUGHTERS OF THE
AMERICAN REVOLUTION,

HUDSON, N. Y.,

For the Benefit of the Chapter Building Fund.

MARY AND I GO TO EUROPE.

Truth, naked, unblushing truth, the first virtue of more serious history, must be the sole recommendation of this personal history.—GIBBON, AUTOBIOGRAPHY.

Travellers never did lie, though fools at home condemn them.—SHAKESPEARE.

WHY THIS BOOK IS PUBLISHED.

To Hendrick Hudson Chapter, Daughters of the American Revolution, of Hudson, N. Y., the world is indebted for the publication of this volume. Later it may blame it. Had it not been for this Society, other eyes than those of intimate friends would never have read its pages. To aid the laudable causes in which the members are engaged, I, Dr. Piller, have consented to the printing and sale of the work, the proceeds to be added to the funds of the Chapter, and used as may be deemed best for furthering its objects. The book, as will easily be seen, makes no pretension to literary merit, unless in those portions quoted from other writers. Its inaccuracies are due to Mary. Much more could have been written concerning what we saw and enjoyed, but it would have stopped the sale of other books, discouraged rising authors, and checked tours to foreign lands. This would have been wrong. The mixture was compounded during office hours, as moments could be stolen from a busy profession, or on Sundays when I should have been at Church. The original volume was struck off on a type-writing machine, and when the manuscript was handed to the printer he was told to "follow copy." This in part may account for many of its shortcomings, its solecisms, and the general mixed up condition of things. What it lacks, and how much better you could have written it, you will know when you have completed the reading. A. P.

TO MARY;

THE BEST OF WIVES, AS WELL AS THE BEST OF

COMPANIONS;

WHETHER OVER LIFE'S STORMY SEA,

OR

IN FOREIGN LANDS.

ALWAYS THE SAFETY-VALVE ON THE BOILER OF

MY ENTHUSIASM,

THIS BOOK

IS

DEDICATED.

PREFACE.

The best books I have read had prefaces. This is no reason why the present volume should have, but it gives the reader more for his money. It may also aid in dispelling the delusion some of my friends have in mind, namely, that my wife *went* with me. I shall speak of my wife often. I call her the "sunshine of my life," because she makes it hot for me. She is part of the book, really the greater part. So when I use the pronoun "I," it means Mary, except when I am in Paris, or pursuing my anatomical or physiological studies. It would not be proper for her to be present at those times.

Mr. Herbert Spencer, in his little book on "Education," (Moral, Intellectual and Physical,) says something like this : "It is a very false idea that benefit arises from cramming history, dates and the like into children's minds. Teach them something that will be of practical value in life. Tell them where their Liver or Eustachian Tubes are situated. They will have more use for the latter knowledge than for the former." Acting on this suggestion, I propose to tell in plain language, not Shakespearian in its style, what we saw. I shall omit all mathematical problems, all histories of war and conquest, all full descriptions of cathedrals, churches and temples, except so far as may be unavoidable. These have been so often and so much better written up than I can do, who am unaccustomed to making books, that the reader will find it to his advantage to hunt up any reference I may make to anything that attracts his interest, if he deems it worth the while to follow the subject, and thus obtain a clearer idea of the situation than I give. The book is written for the entertainment and amusement of our friends. An unvarnished tale, and simple account of our personal experiences in the first and only vacation during my professional life. Some one has said "Life is only worth living for the Summer Vacation." I have found this true. If you doubt me, go as I did.

A. PILLER, Doctor.

Recovery Hall,
  Hudson, N. Y.,
    1898.

P. S. Misspelling is due to the machine. Errors of grammar, capitals and punctuation to ignorance.

CONTENTS.

	PAGE.
PREFACE	7

CHAPTER I.
        Preparations 13

CHAPTER II.
        At Sea.. 22

CHAPTER III.
        At Sea.. 42

CHAPTER IV.
        Gibraltar..................................... 52

CHAPTER V.
        Genoa 60

CHAPTER VI.
        Pisa 70

CHAPTER VII.
        Rome... 82

CHAPTER VIII.
Naples.. 94
Pompeii.. 98

CHAPTER IX.
Florence... 103

CHAPTER X.
Venice... 108
Lido... 115

CHAPTER XI.
Milan.. 118

CHAPTER XII.
Lucerne.. 125

CHAPTER XIII.
Munich... 135

CHAPTER XIV.
Vienna... 145

CHAPTER XV.
Dresden.. 155

CHAPTER XVI.
Berlin... 160
Potsdam.. 167
Sans Souci... 168

CHAPTER XVII.

Frankfort-on-the-Main 172
Heidelburg 174
Mayence 176

CHAPTER XVIII.

The Rhine 179
Cologne 182

CHAPTER XIX.

Amsterdam 186
Haarlem 190
The Hague 192
Scheveningen 194

CHAPTER XX.

Antwerp 196

CHAPTER XXI.

Brussels 201

CHAPTER XXII.

Paris 206
Versailles 214

CHAPTER XXIII.

London 215
Kew 223
Hampton Court 223
Windsor 224
Eton 224

CHAPTER XXIV.

Homeward Bound 227

COPYRIGHT BY
H. LYLE SMITH, M. D.,
HUDSON, N. Y.
OCTOBER,
1898.

MARY AND I GO TO EUROPE.

CHAPTER I.

PREPARATIONS.

"It is the unexpected that happens."

It has always been a mystery to me how I, a country doctor, ever decided to go to Europe. I thought like many others, I could not be spared; that the environment about me and of which I thought I was the axis would cease to revolve; that the whole of Creation would stop, and I should be missed. I have found out otherwise. No man's feet are so large but another's shoes can fill the impressions made in the sands of life's shore, and often fit better than the originals.

I had dug along, following my professional calling with more or less of success for many years; now and then taking a day off, but never a vacation in the true sense of the word. Sometimes curing a case, now and then making a mistake in diagnosis or treatment, or both, filling up with tears and regrets to the family what I felt, and they did not know. I grew tired. The everlasting tales of woe became irritations, and while now and then the monotony was broken by some one paying a long over-due account, while laboring under temporary mental health, this unction did not serve as a substitute for a something I desired, and knew I needed. Like a crisis in a disease the time came. I was taken ill, not severely so, just enough to cause me to relinquish office hours, though I still continued to visit those of my patients who had sufficient confidence in me to refuse being killed by the hands of other practitioners. As the first batch of microbes left, leaving me under the delusion I was convalescing, another swarm came down like an after-dinner course to give zest to the whole. Then my horse ran away and my son was married. To an ordinary mortal these "visitations," or mixtures would have appeared sufficient to warrant a rest, a little easement in labor, a little folding of the hands. I deserved something, anyway. For me, however, they were only ripples, microscopic splashes on the surface of the sea of my life. The cyclone that wrecked my bark, was the putting into execution by my wife, of a house-cleaning plan. I wish to say my wife is no ordinary woman, which fact is borne out by another, namely that she married me. I have often insisted she was the only one of the two who was married, I being simply a guest at the wedding. She cleaned, and had I died during the performance, the funeral would have been held in the yard, as there would have been no room for the corpse in the house. She began with one apartment. This, she said, was all she "intended to do." But, parenthetically, my wife is always cleaning. She has no set legal holiday for it, extending over a week, or more, like other housewives, but appears to do it daily, in fact all the time. On this occasion it was done so thoroughly, every thing when she finished was new, except the land on which the house stood. I was the next older. This insanity settled the business, and I made up my mind I should have to go under the sod, (for which some of my friends said I was not prepared,) leaving her to enjoy my insurance, or get away for the purpose of saving my life. Now it is no easy thing for a man, especially a professional man, to pack up his duds, leave his friends and creditors, shut shop, having no clerks to sell pills in job lots at reduced prices, after he has been moving along in one groove for thirty years. A doctor has a feeling of fear that some other of his clan may get hold of his best paying "chronics" and cure them, thus cutting off a sure and constant revenue. I was afraid of this. On the contrary such a going would be a valid excuse to present bills, in order to find out how much of real love patients have for their family physician.

So the mass of pros and cons were put into the mortar of thought, and ground into the powder of decision. I wanted to go somewhere, most of all to Europe. This I desired for many reasons. Nearly all doctors do. It seems to impress a patient, or a community, if a medical man has put foot into a European hospital he has imbibed some potent influence, not obtainable by any course of study, or bedside experience in this country, which he can exert at will for the benefit of the sick. It sounds well to have "been abroad." Then, too, so many of my friends, just because they knew I probably never could do it, were constantly telling me of the delights of an ocean voyage, "the perfect rest, nothing like it to bring back exhausted vitality, no night calls, no muddy roads," and all that sort of thing. I, so they said, "needed change." I did. And to "brush up against the great minds of my profession." All this and much more, partaking of the same character, decided me. I thought it better than to take a trip in my own country, for did I go to either end of it, as soon as I felt rested I would be sure to return home, and be back at the old job before the desired purpose was accomplished. Another reason, I wanted variety. There is a great difference between rest and repose. One may be merely a change of activities, while the other may be a long drawn exertion. Carlyle, in his Sartor Resartus, goes into the definition of the words, and to his work I refer you for a more lucid explanation of the subject. Travel within my own country meant the same language, the same laws. It would have presented the same orders of architecture, the same customs of the peoples, and though probably I should have been "in cog." to the great mass of my brethren, the handle of "doctor" might now and then have slipped out, and I been called to treat, of course gratuitously, some one who would "remit later on arrival home." My line of battle being decided, I began to look about for my guns. I found I could raise some funds, but how I could expend them to the best advantage was the question. Tourist Agencies were interviewed, consultations held with those who had been partakers of the joys I anticipated. Great divergence of opinion was found, each opinion seeming to depend upon the size of a presumptive Letter of Credit. In fact, one of my friends, a retired physician to whom I went for suggestions, knowing he would tell me the entire truth by reason of the brotherhood, greeted me with, "how much money have you?" After stating the amount I thought I could borrow, he replied, "you can do it." The first gate to the Garden of Pleasure was opened. Complications now began to arise in my home. My wife, who heretofore had enjoyed unusual health, and who had unselfishly insisted I should go alone, by reason of the expenditure entailed, began to present symptoms of decline, at least she said she felt them. To me, as a physician, there were no apparent evidences of physical degeneration. At first I thought the house cleaning had been too much for her, but later surmised she would miss me, that a sort of "Oikeiomania" was setting in. A talk with other married men led me to believe this was not an uncommon state with wives, when husbands threatened to go abroad alone. I reasoned she was beginning to mistrust, or distrust me, and from association with her friends had imbibed largely of "why do you not go too?" Her collapse was stayed by saying, "My dear, a trip to Europe with you not in it, would be a rose without a thorn, or a thorn without a rose," (I have forgotten which) "you too shall go." The reader will find, before he reaches the end of this book, that I went with her. Trouble started in at once. As I slowly contracted the circle of my practice, my wife expanded in the direction of her supposed needs. From bonnets to shoes, every article that could or might be required in a three months' visit was priced and samples obtained. Of course, according to her idea, nothing could be bought in Europe. At least, my wife endeavored to fix in my mind what she believed to be a fact. My own wardrobe was simplicity itself, including celluloid collars. They, celluloid collars, pay, not only in money, but in comfort. If ever you go, don't forget to take half a dozen. I did not, my wife did. I'll tell you how this happened. A married daughter living in New York, had been presented by an admiring friend with a pair of embroidered pillow cases. My wife's economy led her to hold the articles in stock until a convenient season when she should go to the city taking them with her, thus saving freight, or expressage. This was her opportunity. So the cases were carefully packed in our single trunk to be delivered to the rightful owner on reaching the great city. They were eventually. Only this happened between. My celluloid collars were left at home, while the cases traveled all over Europe in their place. I used the cases as a substitute for a remembrance of the other side, and my daughter still admires the handiwork of Parisian needlewomen. I have learned it is a wise act to go through your trunk after your wife has said she has packed it, especially when going abroad. Another thing I would suggest: either buy, or invent a trunk that will lock and unlock itself, merely by kicking or swearing at it. In our journey I opened that small piece of baggage of ours over a million of times, perhaps more, but I'm safe on a million. If you have put down, or mislaid anything, or suppose you have lost it, from a hair pin to a relic, your wife will say it is in the trunk and order you to look for it. You know it is not there, but you'll be fool enough to do it, or afraid to disobey. Ninety and nine times out of a hundred it will not be in it, as you know. I've had an experience with that trunk which, if applied to my profession, would make me a professor in a medical college. The next time I go, I shall take a hand bag and my character, nothing else.

The day of departure, the eventful day at last arrived. Being in length of service, the oldest practitioner in my little city, the good-byes, partook somewhat of a public character. The press had mentioned our intended going as an item of news and interest. The local military company turned out, saluted me and wished me *bon-voyage* in true soldierly style. Little gifts came to us from loving hearts, torpedoes were placed upon the railroad track to boom us on as we left the station; so amid a blaze of glory, mingled with kisses from my wife's dearest friends, of which I took as large a portion as I could, we rolled away, leaving my home, nearly three thousand of the inhabitants of which I had ushered into the world, and the cemetery, where nearly——— thousands had been helped to a permanent resting place through my efforts. As a last act, I confided my patients to Nature and quack compounds, and started for the grand event of my existence.

It is said "the three great events of human life are birth, marriage, and death." I have been through two of them, but never enjoyed either so much as the anticipations before me. I got what did not occur in the other two. As for the last, that remains to be seen, or felt. My pastor thinks the question an open one as yet. He and I do not agree on certain theological constructions. He, in my opinion, has too much faith, that is now. I hope to convert him to my way of looking at facts.

We arrived in New York two days before the expected sailing of the ship. This was done that my wife might price more samples and job lots of goods, for which she had no earthly need, and that I might look around in order to become acquainted with "ways that were dark." I was not sure but a little experience in this line would work in well on the other side. I bought Baedekers, a letter of credit, a corkscrew and a lot of other useless things I supposed would come handy. I could have purchased more celluloid collars had I known the contents of that blank trunk. I also took occasion, the day before we sailed, to visit the vessel, look her over and form my opinion of the captain, to whom I had a letter of introduction. A bottle of champagne during the voyage, beats all written communications out of sight. This I learned from the application of both methods of acquaintance.

CHAPTER II.

AT SEA.

"Merrily we sail along o'er the deep blue sea."

SATURDAY, the day of separation from our native land, broke unadulterate. We could not have picked a riper one for the month of May had we searched the almanac. It is needless to say we awoke early so as to get on board in time. Here began the first of misstatements. We read on our tickets, "passengers are required to be on board one hour before sailing." This is not true. If you are on deck at any time before the boat leaves quarantine you may go, provided your ticket is paid for.

The usual number of friends came to the pier to say farewell, and kiss my wife. Flowers and oranges there were for her in abundance. For me, telegrams, one of the most interesting of which read, "best wishes for a safe voyage; if you get short of funds draw on me." Now that had the true spirit, and as this particular one came from the president of the largest and so far safest bank in my town, it was more than gratifying. I did not, however, call on him. He saved his cake and credit nevertheless, by the offer. I shall return the compliment should he ever go, that is, so far as the "wishes" are concerned. As to the second clause, I shall think it over. He might want bail. You can never tell about these bank officials, they go suddenly, sometimes. One of my dearest friends, a lady, had the forethought to present me with a diary, to which I daily devoted a few moments and kept a few notes, except when in Paris. No one has time in Paris to keep anything, except his respectability. I shall, therefore, take the liberty of quoting from these original pages the history of our outward passage, adding such thoughts and morals as come to mind, or promise to be of service to others when in a similar situation.

Our ship, (every one who goes to sea uses the possessive case) the "Werra," Capt. Pohle, one of the North German Lloyds great fleet, was bound for Genoa, with no stops between, so far as advertised, except at Gibraltar. She was the best boat in which I had ever crossed the Atlantic. In my travels I have met many who have sailed by other lines, and have yet to find one who does not speak in the highest terms of the comfort, cuisine and seamanship offered by this company to sea-going people. This is not an advertisement for the N. G. L's, nor do I expect a rebate when I go with them again, as I certainly hope to do.

We got away from the pier, at last, by the aid of two tugs, much sobbing and weeping, the band playing, colors flying and the usual *éclat* that adheres to such an event. I suppose it takes place regularly twice a week the year round, but to us it was novel, never having been in a like predicament. Our journey had begun in reality and my wife to have her innings. I think it is Emerson who says, "in a tour abroad there is three per cent. of expectation, two per cent. of realization and five per cent. of recollection." In our case, at least, this needs modification. We expected less than we realized, realized more than we expected, and as the spool of recollection and memory unwinds the thread of the past, we find those days were a glorious prison house, where love was jailor and the bars delight. My wife, soon after leaving port, went below to her room to "regulate things." It was hard to break up an old habit. I remained on deck to see what was going on. We had aboard, as I found later, the usual types, or class of passengers. The man who was making his 66th voyage, the fellow who wished he had not come, the man who never lost a meal, he who was not hungry, the Kodak fiend, the Captain's terror, and the blushing bride.

I had been aboard but a few hours when I thought I knew the ship by heart. I had investigated every part of it, except the furnace room and the crow's nest, where the look-out is supposed to be stationed, though this I did later. Everything was, as a friend of mine who was once in the drug business invariably stated, "a new novelty," laden with surprises, if not with experiences and information. I chanced early in the day to stray into the smoke room, a place I afterwards found fraught with stories, good times and naps. I shall speak of it again. Here I encountered a jolly crowd tasting, or testing the dark product of Munich. As I knew I should be brought later face to face with the same, I deemed it wise to make an experiment under the noses of those I judged were more learned in the matter than I. I am a temperance man at home, but when traveling, I fear change of water and do as others do. I do not like to insult a country by declining its chief food products. I ordered a glass of the beverage, at the same time handing the waiter my last American half dollar. He was gone some time, so long, I began to think he had run off with my funds, yet felt satisfied he could go no further than I, so would "see him later." He returned, and I thought I understood the cause of the delay. It was not the size of the glass, but the amount of change. At first I thought he had brought up part of the cargo; then that he had mistaken my half for a gold fifty. At any rate, I drank my bier in haste, lest he should discover his mistake, and went below to find Mary (that is my wife's name.) She was in the stateroom "regulating." I proceeded to tell her of my stroke in finance and suggested if she had no objections I'd stick to bier, as it would save using our letter of credit and enable me to retire from practice on my return. She asked to see what had been given me as change, and as there were no bargain counters, or auctions on board, I felt it safe to trust her with the funds. Mary has a mathematical mind, and after a few moments spent in looking over the ballast, quietly said, "You old —— (she used a monosyllable) the change is correct and you have paid twice as much for the bier as you do at home." I changed the subject, but got even with the steward by spending all the freight he had given me on the same lines as produced it. Before I left, Mary informed me she had discovered a place for swearing. She knew it was for that purpose, as it was labeled "Für Damen." She also said if I felt aggrieved at the bar-tender, it would be a good plan to go into it and settle the matter with him then and there. Mary was not as proficient in the German language as she was later.

My diary says:

MAY 23, *Saturday.*—"I wish it were possible to frame into words or speech the emotions I feel. That I were a painter for the sake of the sweet picture. I seem to have lost hold of everything. Where am I, I asked myself this morning as we sailed away, the old "Ego" is no longer present.

To think, for me, there are to be days and weeks of rest, pleasure and freedom. That I may sit down and dictate, command and not be commanded. What a delicious dream it is. To think I may sleep; lay myself down in the belief I shall rest undisturbed till morning breaks, which I have not done in more than thirty years. Did sweeter flowers ever bloom, were music's strains ever more harmonious than this thought? Strange are my feelings. I walk about the deck, as it were in the third person, wondering by what enchantment I havebeen disembodied. I am not myself. My wife is at my side, and we seem to be looking backward, down the avenue of the past and feel as if the days of youth have come again. We are like children let loose from school, thinking only of the pleasures held in store in the hours beyond.

....As the land recedes further and further from our sight, the air grows cold. We don our wraps and thicker clothing. Luncheon has been served and dinner eaten. No qualms of Mal de Mer. The vessel rolls not unpleasantly, a sort of rocking, as if the sea wished to add to our enjoyment.

My studies in the prevention of sea-sickness, which I pursued with more zest than I did some other types of ailments, seeing my wife and I were to be the patients, had brought forth no satisfactory results. Numerous remedies, I found were suggested by those who had had an actual experience, and many more, by those teachers who wrote on the subject, reasoning from a theory. I decided to let the whole thing alone, trusting to luck, and if anything turned up to go at it on the "expectant" plan, that is, to treat ourselves as symptoms and circumstances arose. I think I did wisely. My advice would be, to those contemplating a voyage, don't bother about "preventives." Eat moderately for a few days before going abroad, especially on the day of sailing, and, if possible, skip a meal or two on the auspicious date. The temptations of the lunch and dinner tables the first day out are, as a rule, too much for the average man or woman to withstand, and indulgence pays tribute to Neptune the following morning, if not before. Another thing, go on board well dressed. Do not think any old rag is good enough for the ship. You will be brought into contact with cultivated people, ladies and gentlemen, and the impression you make at first, lasts through the entire voyage. In a day or two you may put on a less fashionable or more worn out costume, and lay the Sunday apparel away till you step on shore again. If you are seasick, you won't care about dress. You'll sigh for wings, and harps and crowns. I have heard it said of a Frenchman, that at first he was afraid he would die, and later he feared he could not. I've seen those I thought were in this second stage.

The people one meets aboard ship are of all kinds and shapes. We had them. The Priest going to Rome for a little more Apostolic succession. The Rabbi who was pointed toward Palestine to find out the cause for the Talmud. The pretty girl (chaperoned by a near relative) who flirted with all the officers, making their life miserable, apparently, by climbing onto the bridge and asking "what kind of weather shall we have to-morrow?" The man of business, the bevy of young (?) ladies, going in a "conducted" party, eight-tenths of whom were maidens, one-tenth married, and the balance eligible.

Among such a crowd as this, it was not reasonable to expect I should pass myself off as a married man. So as intimacies grew thicker and more numerous, I introduced my better half as my mother, leading the unsophisticated to believe that she (my wife) was a widow, and I her only son. This gave me a freedom unattainable by other means. To be sure, my beard was sprinkled with grey, a hair or two here and there, (I shaved it off when I reached Paris,) but this represented experience, not age, at least in my case.

To some the hours drag wearily on board ship, and they wish they were ashore. This is "because they have no resources within themselves," as my wife says. I find she is correct when they are sea-sick. The "resources" are all overboard. Most of the daylight and a large part of the night is spent in eating. You have coffee and rolls in your stateroom before you are up, then breakfast. A little later, more refreshments. Before luncheon something to eat, then you lunch. In the afternoon beef, chicken, or clam broth, with sandwiches and other truck. Then dinner. This is the "She Dove" of the day. You come to the table, that is, if you are able, arrayed in the best you have, and begin with soup and end with toothpicks. A real table d'hote well cooked, well served, a menu card at your hand, a waiter at your back, and an orchestra at the foot of the companion way. What do you want more? You eat about two hours and then go into the smoke-room to get something to satisfy your hunger. Here you indulge in sandwiches and a bottle of something, or a glass of cordial. During all this performance of the day, you are supposed to patronize the waiter in the smoke-room, and become acquainted with the liquid supplies of the ship. A man, if he is any kind of a stevedore, can unload about twenty schooners between sunrise and bedtime. After my first experience I bought a bier-card, a little machine filled with numbers, one of which the waiter punches out every time you order a prophylactic. I found it less awkward than waiting for change, and I got my medicine sooner. To be sure, it uses itself up rapidly, but what are you on a vacation for? If you go with the idea you can save money, it would be better for you to remain at home. When one is not eating, or punching out holes in the bier-card, "Shovel Board" may be played. There is nothing like this game on earth. The nearest resemblance is Croquet, and that has no similarity whatever to it. One of the crew chalks out on the deck a program, something like this:

8	1	6
3	5	7
4	9	2

with numbers in each space. In this instance I may have them properly placed, probably not. I don't think it makes a great deal of difference how they are lodged, so long as they are all in the scheme. The imbeciles who attempt to play at it, stand off fifteen or twenty feet, and with a long stick, like a billiard mace, broad at the distal end and covered with leather, so as not to scratch the deck, strive to shove a wooden disk, eight inches in diameter by an inch thick onto one of the numbered spots in the figure. Sides are arranged, and the partners who get the greatest number of tricks in a certain number of shoves win the pot. I did not play it often.

Mother did not care to have me exert myself, as I was out for a rest. Then the other side always had all the prettiest girls, and it used up my card too rapidly. You are obliged to cool off so often, you know, and your partners cool with you. I think I came out ahead of the game only once during the voyage of twelve days. I did not play it coming home.

Then there are rings made of rope, which you insanely attempt to pitch over the end of a stick. This delights some more than others. It made one youngster happy, who was aboard in care of a nurse. I never saw the mother as I remember. The kid tried to pitch the hempen circles ashore by throwing them into the sea. He did me a kindness without knowing it. Some read, or strive to make you believe they are reading. When we started, we intended to do the same in regard to all the places we expected to visit. We didn't do it, at least I did not. My wife made several trials at it, but was interrupted so often by mealtime she gave it up in the end. I was too busy eating and fooling with that bier-card to waste time on literature. The deck is a great place to snooze. Hand your card to the waiter, take without question what he brings you, (you are safe,) wrap yourself up in your rug, lie down in your chair just out of the sun's rays, shut your eyes, forget your creditors and go to sleep. When you wake up, it will be time to eat, or to send down your card. Under this treatment mother lost twelve, and I gained twenty pounds of solid adipose before we reached Gibraltar. This speaks well for the ozone in the air, and the absence of microbes in the bier. Mother says "microbes know better than to get into bier." She is prejudiced, and sticks to Rhine wine and champagne. There are microbes in the last mentioned article I know, for I have felt them in my head the next morning.

So the day is whiled away. You keep count of the bells and wonder what is the trouble with your watch. As you are not always sure whether it is eight o'clock in the morning, or four in the afternoon, you decide to have it cleaned at the first opportunity. Or you listen to the bugle-boy making alleged music. They never call you to meals aboard a steamship, or ring a bell, they *blow* you there. Now and then the instrument slips a cog, but if you have no ear for music, or do not know the tune, you will think it is all right. The bugle-boy always begins what he regards as a concert, half an hour before the meal is served. This is to allow you to dress, or work your card.

Now and then the outline of a vessel is sighted, far off on the border of where sky and water meet. Everyone wastes time in trying to read her name, or guess the line to which she belongs. It is usually a failure. They try to measure the length of the smoke seen issuing from the stacks.

This meets with the same success. Flying fish and Mother Cary's chickens add to the interesting data of the day. Porpoises skip and jump about the ship, making the mind wonder what sort of apparatus they have inside that enables them to keep pace with the boat. A whale is seen spouting two or three ship's lengths ahead, or at the side, and everybody rushes to the rail to catch a glimpse. They are scarce on land. At night, the phosphorescence attracts the attention. After reading "The Ancient Mariner," I was somewhat disappointed in the display. Some look at the moon and romance to the pretty girl at their side, that is, if the party of the first part happens to be unmarried, as I was for the time.

A night at sea, with the moon shining at its full, the firmament sparkling with its myriads of stars, beats all the living pictures I have ever seen. One falls into a meditative mood. You look out into this great universe, of which the earth is so small a speck that, as some astronomer says, "were the strongest telescope known planted upon one of the nearest planets, and the whole expanse of the heavens searched, this earth of ours might easily escape notice, so small it is." Then as you give reins to thought, contemplating the greatness of it all, then coming back to earth, great even in its comparative smallness, then to the mighty ocean on which you are sailing, then to the ship, a dot in the immensity of waters, last to yourself, an atom in the huge vessel, you ask yourself, "what am I?" How small, indeed, you are, and yet you kick up a row if anything goes wrong. Do this gazing and meditating for a week, and you'll think less of yourself and more of the world at large. You'll begin to realize that you were made for this earth, rather than the world for you. I know no better treatment to take the conceit out of a man who thinks mundane affairs unable to get along without him. It took it out of me.

Often before the hour of retiring, the captain of the ship on our outward voyage converted the upper decks into a ball-room, by festooning the sides with flags of all nations, electric lights and other adornments. Those older than ourselves gave an exhibition of what the "two-step" should be. In this way the days rolled by, days all too short. We imagined when we started, two weeks at sea would be a long time. We were surprised the hours passed so quickly. We even found we had left quite a number of things undone when we got ashore, but trusted the Deck Steward would look after the remains. By the by, this fellow is the hardest worked man on the ship except the passenger who is sea-sick. His duties involve everything but steering and shoveling coal. They would put him at these on a pinch. It shall be my habit to give him five dollars every time I go over. This trip I thought four marks sufficient. What does he do? Ask what he is called upon not to do. Do you wish a chair, do you wish it changed to another spot, do you wish to buy, sell, find anything, he is the man to do it. Nothing is out of his province and he does it all willingly, asking no other favor at your hands, than love, sweet looks, and a mark.

When we went aboard at New York we did not know one of the most important first steps was to secure seats at the table. The one falling to your lot you hold during the passage. We had been told all about it, but there was so much to remember, a little thing like this was easily forgotten. It is the 2d Steward's business to attend to it and we let him. Whether the handle to my name, as it appeared on the passenger list, or the winning ways of my wife, caught without her knowledge, had any telepathic influence, I know not, anyhow we were placed at the table of the ship's surgeon, my wife in the seat of honor at his right. The captain held audience at the other end of the bar, *vis-a-vis* to the doctor. I have always been glad he forgot that letter of introduction, else we might have been seated at his end, and been prevented from running that portion of the craft at which we were; in fact we ran the entire room after a few days. Sitting opposite, so as to face us, were two gentlemen returning to Bremen via Genoa, after a long business residence in Samoa. A short acquaintance with the younger convinced my wife he was a lunatic, and she has held this opinion ever since. My diagnosis was "mere boyishness." The shackles of constraint had been thrown off and he was in for a good time and he had it. We helped him. At each meal we made new acquaintances, my wife giving her attention to those at the opposite side of our table, while I bestowed my favors on the ladies at my left.

At the first meal, luncheon, I discovered near my plate a bottle of Claret wine. My wife has always insisted it was *not* near. I accepted the situation and what was apparently an invitation, supposing it a gift from the captain, as he had my letter of introduction, or was one of the customs of the ship. In spite of my wife's "don't do it, you had better be careful, it may not be intended for you," I took the chances. I am a veteran of the late war and married, so by reason of past experiences could afford to run some risks. I drank it. Later I found I had robbed the doctor. He did not happen to be at this repast, probably being detained in his office, or in the steerage, where countless Italian immigrants were stowed, or was out in the country making calls. I squared the account with him in a day or two by putting up the wine, and I rather think he would enjoy being waylaid again. It was like a lover's quarrel, so nice to make up. After a few sit-downs with us at meals, he was never absent. I sometimes thought he neglected his patients to be with us.

Our end of the boat kept up with the procession, and left enough fun behind to run the Damfer back to New York. In eating, I am not fond of too much style, I rather favor a free and easy method.

The berths on a first-class steamship are arranged for economy, not on the score of comfort, or for real use. It is all very well to live in a two-story flat, but I object to going under the roof to sleep at night. Our room was one of the best on the plan, chosen for us by our son-in-law, who had sailed all over the world and knew a good room when he saw it. It was well forward on the port side and furnished with electric lights, hot and cold water, bells, a lounge and a window looking out to the other end of the world. As compared to the size of my wife it was small, so I always allowed her to retire first. This gave me more time in the smoke-room to eat, and more latitude and longitude when I came to disrobe. As she was usually first in bed, she always took the lower shelf, compelling me to mount by ladder to the realms above. When the storm set in, as it did the second day out, I threw away the steps, and climbed in on a sort of go as you please plan. It was easier, and I got to bed sooner. These roosts are anything but certain. You are up, or out, sometimes before you are called, though the rule is, not to move till the bugle-boy toots his horn in the morning about six bells. A bath, followed by a good breakfast, starts the day in proper shape. Sunday at sea passes like any other day. The same every thing happens. On some lines they hold a religious service in the morning for those who have no future prospects, and take up a collection. We held none going out, as we were too busy looking for next week. One congregation of the passengers I admire. That is the concert given for the benefit of the widows and orphans of sailors. While we held no concert, here and there about the lower deck were boxes marked as receptacles for funds for this laudable object. I never saw one entirely empty, and he is a mighty mean fellow who will not drop a nickel into the slot for this worthy charity. As to price, these concerts are highly artistic. For the performance no charge is made, it is the program you pay for. The Chief Steward is, as a rule, the whole show, and as his songs and jokes are always new to those who have not heard them, he is at times entertaining. Now and then a "Star" happens to be on board, and after much solicitation he, or she "consents" to do an act, or favor the crowd with a "selection." They get their names conspicuously printed on the program and free through this act of self-denial.

We were never sick in the least degree. Many times and oft we counseled over the matter, thinking it was the proper thing to do, and that the hour had arrived. Only the crew, and ourselves, kept well. This looked unfashionable and below the average culture of our fellows. Even in the days of the storm we held our own in every sense. The English channel did not disturb us, so we think we have had our baptism, and that it took.

Before we reached Genoa, I went down into the engine and furnace rooms, the great lungs and heart of the vessel. What a wonderful place it was, and hot. The engineer told me some immense tales about the amount of coal consumed on a voyage, the waste of water, and the cost of his department, all of which I am inclined to believe. I cannot contradict him, as I know nothing about running a steamship, I cannot even run my own family. When we reached Genoa, the vessel stood five feet more out of water than when we left the home port. This in a ship of over six thousand tons showed how large a part of the load had been consumed in pushing us over. Perhaps some of the buoyancy was due to the consumption of bier cards. The stokers look like hardy fellows, yet I understand are short-lived. How they manage to stand the intense exertion and heat of the fires is a mystery to me. There is no loafing among them while on duty. They attend strictly to business and shovel I know not how many tons of coal into those white hot throats during the four hours each gang is at its trick. The rapid changes of temperature to which they are subjected must show their effects in some debility of important organs. It is a hard life at best, but I presume they enjoy it, or would take to the practice of medicine.

My diary ends on the first day as follows:—

".... Quite tired to-night, both retire at 10 P. M."

CHAPTER III.

"Rough winds do shake the darling buds of May."

My diary continues as follows:

MAY 24th, *Sunday morning.*—".... Saturday ended like a dream. We retired in the hope of an enjoyable to-morrow. About two A. M. we were awakened by the sound of the fog-horn, which continued its unearthly noise for an hour. We fell asleep after a while, in spite of a peculiar motion in our beds. On arising in the morning we found a heavy sea, the wind dead ahead and the ship pitching terribly. Breakfast showed a diminution in the number of guests at table from the evening before. We are in the Gulf-stream. The decks are wet and slippery from the spray. The bugle-boy opened the day with "Nearer my God to Thee," and many thought it was so. The vessel rolls so much that it is impossible to keep on the lines while writing in my book. We remain well, take in all the meals and all that is printed on the menu card. Every circumstance is trying. We brace up to it however and shall try to get through the day."....

I noticed while on deck the evening previous to the date of the above, the moon presented a rather singular appearance. It was surrounded by a most gorgeous ring and seemed out for a lark, in a word it looked "full." I did not then appreciate the entire meaning of this astronomical objective symptom. Experience has led me to keep my eye on "Luna" when I am at sea, and I think I can now foretell a gale with as much certainty as the Meteorological Bureau. I sometimes call my wife "Luna." I also learned something about the barometer. Our machine hung over the stair-way to the main saloon. It was an innocent looking affair, but attracted more interest and made more trouble than anything on board, for a day or two at least. It was so cased in, it was impossible for any of us to get at the machinery. Had we been able, we would have had fair weather the entire trip. It was a good deal like the thermometer of the old lady, who said, "it would be hotter if the thermometer were longer."

We took our bearings, (that is the ship's.) to-day at noon. This is done on the "Bridge" by the captain and some other fellows. We found we were at sea and had run 330 nautical miles since twelve o'clock yesterday. A chart, hanging in the companion-way, marks the course we are supposed to be following, and after each daily observation a little flag is stuck in at the proper point to show those interested how far the boat has sailed, and where things are at. It is a frequent diversion in the smoke-room to wager on the number of knots rolled off by the ship daily. I have known men to win sufficient to pay for their bier-cards, staterooms and all other necessary expenses. Then I have encountered those who, by their faces, I judged, wished they had not bet. I never indulge in games of chance, as I have found my practice in its results something of the same sort, uncertain.

MAY 25th, *Monday*.—"The sea still heavy, raining. We pitch and roll more than yesterday, but keep well. We think we should be ill, as it seems the proper thing to do. The captain, Mary and myself only at the breakfast table. It is a bad day. The picture over the desk in my office, (it is one of a steamship on a placid sea) is a snare and a delusion to tempt innocent people out onto this terrible deep. .... The captain says he never met such a wind on this route at this season. We agree. The frames were put on the table to-day." These "frames" are little fences fastened about the space allotted you at table, to prevent the cups, plates and other hardware from getting into your neighbor's yard, or into your lap. They do not always fulfill their mission, as the foundations of the house, in time of storm, have a tendency to change places with the roof. If you don't slop over yourself, your viands are apt to.

May 26th, *Tuesday*.—"Wind has shifted to our quarter .... we roll and roll. Everthing has broken loose in our room, and I am black and blue from the bumps and bruises I get walking about. Why did I leave home? I want no better evidence that a man is a d—— fool than to know he has crossed the Atlantic .... During the night the water broke through the glass covering of the engine-room, flooding it. It also carried away some stanchions and deck-chairs. In the words of Mary's imperfect Italian, we had a 'helophatyme'."

During this little playspell of the Atlantic, many amusing incidents occurred. This morning I was sitting on the edge of my bunk, Mary directly opposite on the lounge attending to some arrangement of her apparel, when a more than usually large wave, just as if the sea were trying to show us what it could do, struck the side of the ship. With an intensity and vim Mary had not shown toward me for years, she rushed into my arms, knocking me into the back of the berth. I thought I had gone through the side of the ship. Then, with the next roll of the vessel, having done all the damage possible, she was thrown back to the lounge, where she found herself seated as before the performance. It was a most ridiculous affair. This same day I injured my arm so as to cause me much annoyance during our entire trip. In fact it did not recover its natural condition until some months after my return home. I found out what the sea could do. By some mistake of my wife .... (she always laid the blame on me; perhaps she is correct,) the port-hole of our room was left insecurely fastened. The result was, while at breakfast the sea burst it open and flooded the apartment. It ruined my wife's traveling dress, made the room steward swear, and spoiled my hat. I straightened out matters in Paris, by buying one of those millinery creations called a woman's bonnet.

The only advantage I can see in a storm on the ocean, one that makes the boat roll in good style, is, that a fellow may get full, lose all power of muscular co-ordination and then lay his inability to walk to the motion. Your best friend would not know you were off. It affects the language as well as the legs. Another thing: I never before appreciated the power and the weight of water. As we lay in our berths we heard the immense waves fall upon the deck above us, as though a thousand trip-hammers were striking in unison. Then we felt ourselves go down, down, down, under the enormous load, as if we were being pushed to the bottom. Then the struggle for life seemed to begin, the ship endeavoring to reach the surface for one more gasp of air, slowly up, up it came. You hear the water swash and fall from off the decks and you breathe again. So on and on it keeps, till it grows monotonous. Mary paid no attention to it. She slept.

May 27th, *Wednesday.*—"A very quiet night (comparatively.) Wind and sea gone down. I have my idea of the man who wrote, 'A life on the ocean wave.' .... Band played on deck for the first since leaving port."

May 28th, *Thursday*—".... a beautiful morning. Some wind, the ship continues to roll: all sails set to steady her .... more people at breakfast .... hope to see the Azores to-morrow and reach Genoa a week from to-day....."

The real fun began at this date.

May 29th, *Friday.*—"More sea on; windy, but warm. Have not as yet experienced that 'smooth as glass and mill-pond' state of things. The bugle-boy awakened us with 'Life let us cherish', and we begin to do so .... About 7 o'clock, A. M., caught sight of the Azore islands and at 10:30 A. M., passed between the first two Las Flores, the larger, on the starboard, and El Cabo on the port side. They appear fertile and several small collections of houses presenting the appearance of villages may be seen at the base of the high cliffs. The remainder of the group was passed by during the night."

The dinner to-day was an "event." In some mysterious way the doctor, and the gentlemen at our end of the table, thought a birthday for my wife was due. Through a still more mysterious influence, the birthday got hold of the wrong person. Anyhow, the presents, illuminations and friendly greetings were taken in by "the only son." Unknown to my wife or to *me*, the doctor, the "Lunatic" and the other rascals had interviewed the cook, and by gifts, promises, threats, or all combined, had enlisted him in the scheme they proposed to work out. Near the middle of the repast, the electric lights were turned out, and the head waiter, followed by a train of his satellites, marched slowly down the aisle, bearing in his hands a large cake on which sixteen colored candles were burning. The cake was a monument to the confectioner's art. Upon the frosting were the words formed from sugar, "sweet sixteen," "many happy returns." Small American and German flags and ensigns garnished it, woven in among silver leaves and golden flowers. Altogether it was a thing of beauty .... outside. Then there was placed at my hand a large basket of flowers made from turnips, potatoes, and other vegetables, also a bouquet of the same materials. When the gifts had been located, the electric lights were turned on, the orchestra played, and I ordered the wine. Congratulations were indulged in, the captain not being forgotten in the bumpers. There was no question as to the odor of the flowers. Nothing remained but to eat the cake. Naturally mother was requested to cut it. There was a good deal of hesitation on her part as she was not sure what the "Lunatic," and the rest of the asylum had in store for her. However, as courage is one of her virtues, she dared the lion and brought from the interior a somewhat heterogeneous mixture of excelsior, old rope and shavings. Of course the play of words, the toasts and the general good feeling added what I am unable to describe. Every one in the cabin wished he were at our end of the table.

I was a good deal surprised at the Azores. Not only at them, but at all the islands seen. Whether I did not know, or had forgotten, their general character startled me. I remember reading in my Geography that an island was "a parcel of land surrounded by water." This still holds good in one sense, but it does not tell the entire truth. What astonished me was, they stuck so far out of water. All the islands I had ever seen were flat, here and there a hill, but these oceanic periods were higher than they were broad. I knew volcanic action had much to do with their formation, yet had no idea they held such high and lofty aspirations. You learn much by getting away from home.

MAY 30th, *Saturday.*—".... This being Decoration Day in the States, celebration was in order.... The tables were ornamented in great shape, and each lady presented with a number of American, German and Bremen flags. The orchestra played national melodies. At night a grand ball on the promenade deck, dancing being kept up till six bells (11 o'clock)."

MAY 31st, *Sunday*.—".... The band playing in the saloon awoke us .... The barometer has fallen. That is, the hand has moved back. The box is in the same old spot .... a beautiful day ....."

After dinner those who did not know how to read gathered aft, and sang sacred songs, those who did, congregated in the library, or lady's cabin on the upper deck. There were many good voices, and at times it was the least disagreeable of the many noises about. This was kept up till the mental hymn books were exhausted, when most of the artists went to bed. A few congenial spirits met in the smoke-room and proceeded to have opera. One of the gentlemen possessed a most charming voice which had been cultivated under some of the best teachers of Italy. I was born a baritone, at least I think I was, but on this occasion I took the bass. We had about two hours at it, with fair prospects of a longer season, when the whole trip was broken up by my wife sending the room steward to see if I were aboard. I sent back word I was, and intended to stick by the ship till we had had the worth of our tickets. This did not satisfy her. Two additional trips were made by her lackey. In order that I might have peace the next day, I broke up the combination and went below. It was a severe shock and disappointment to me, for it was the only real opportunity I have ever had of letting a real artist hear the quality of my voice, that is in the line of opera.

JUNE 1st, *Monday.*—"The most lovely day of all. At 12 M. passed by Cape St. Vincent, the western point of Portugal ...., with its forts and signal stations .... We are now constantly meeting ships and steamers coming from southern ports .... To-morrow, Gibraltar...."

As there was a chance of meeting mail facilities at the Rock, I spent several hours of the day writing letters home. To the children, to "the only woman I ever loved," and others. It seemed strange to stick a stamp on the envelope that did not bear the image of George Washington. Nevertheless it evidently had a right of way, for all my epistles reached their destination.

Before sailing I purchased a fountain pen under the delusion that the thing would do as the advertisement said. It did more. It squirted the ink over my fingers, onto the paper and ruined the carpet. The thing it would not do, was write. After reasonable attempts to get my invested value out of it, I took up with the belaying pins furnished by the company. When I arrived in London, I gave the alleged pen to a dear friend, telling him how useful it was, and that he would be astonished at its performance. I have no doubt he was. I also told him not to be in a hurry to thank me, or to write with it till I got out of England, as then it would call me to his mind. I've not heard from him since.

CHAPTER IV.

GIBRALTAR.

"Praise the sea, but keep on land ...... "

THE ship dropped anchor in the harbor before Gibraltar last night at 12 P. M. Mary and I were on deck to see the act. The atmosphere was hazy, so as to dim the outline of the structure, but we recognized it as a big thing. Lights were all about the shore and we could hear the sentry call "all's well." Early in the morning (6:30,) when I went above, I found the ship surrounded by bumboats, and the deck taken possession of by vendors, who sold merchandise of the poorest quality at the most exorbitant prices. As the ship's larder needed additions, ample time was given for a trip to shore. Of this I availed myself. My wife decided not to go, as the means of transportation in her eyes was not sufficiently safe. I paid the price, something like half a dollar christian money, and got under way. These tenders seem insignificant affairs after a sail on a big ship, and look as if they would topple over, or go to the bottom on the least provocation. This one was quite as good as any I have since met.

I have never been received anywhere with more enthusiasm than I was on landing at this spot. In fact, before I landed, not even at the Grand Central Station in New York, where every man asks me to "have a hack." Before the tender reached the wharf, I was seized by the natives, dragged on shore and had it not been for my perfect knowledge of Spanish profanity, I might not have lived to write this history. I speak Spanish well, if I say it myself, having lived many years among Cubans and acquiring the lingo as does a child, with nothing omitted. They, consequently, took me to be as great a rascal as they were themselves and let me go. What a motley population it was gathered there at the landing! English, Spanish, Moors, people from all climes and from everywhere under the sun. I remember, particularly, one fellow, a Moor, a magnificient specimen of a man in his physique. He looked as if he had just stepped out from a laundry, his black legs shining like polished marble, the white sheet about him—that is what it appeared to be, immaculate in its color. One of our party attempted to snap a Kodak at him, but whether it proved a success or not, I never learned. I could see the sneer in his face as if he were saying, "You Christian dog, how dare you?"

The wharf was filled with vendors of every conceivable thing on earth. Flowers, strawberries, photographs, fans, laces, shawls, heaven only knows what not, and for which the most exorbitant charges were made. I at once bought a photographic album of the rock, and some fans, fearing the supply might give out. Had I been cooler and had the sense to wait until the tender turned its nose toward the ship, I could have bought at one-tenth the price. For a lot of lying, theiving rascals these fellows beat any bandits I ever met. The Venetians are bank cashiers compared to them. We took a carriage, that is a couple of us boys, and visited the principal points of interest. Before you pass over the bridge, which is at the entrance of the town, you are given a little ticket which reads:

"WATERPORT.—Permit until first evening gun.
    WILLIAM SEED, *Chief of Police.*"

This lets you in.

One is struck with the peculiar features of everything. Soldiers marching and walking about; the narrow streets, some with sidewalks and some without; the donkeys ladened with panniers holding the produce for the markets; the goats being milked before the doors; the signs above the shops, in a language unintelligible to most travelers; people walking, or hurrying to and fro, types of every nation on earth. Now you hear English spoken, then Spanish, then French, now some other tongue, known or unknown. It is a veritable Tower of Babel and an unmistakable den of thieves.

I shall not attempt to describe the Rock. You can learn all about it in any geography, and of its vicissitudes in any fairly and unbiased written history. They claim it is three miles in length, three-quarters of a mile in average breadth, and 1439 feet high above the sea. They lie so here I did not go up to prove it. The aspect of the Rock itself is uninviting, the whole appearing devoid of trees and verdure. About the base heliotrope grows in the wildest luxuriance, perfuming the air and mitigating the other prevailing and less enjoyable odors. The most interesting objects are, the Great Market, the Moorish Castle the Almeda Gardens, Europa, General Eliott's monument, and the Galleries. Into these latter we were permitted to go, though not to a great extent. No Kodak was allowed, so our government must be content with guesses of its interior strength, rather than with plans taken on the spot.

I do not consider it any earthly use for the United States to figure on capturing it and taking it over to Hawaii. England claims she owns it and has fastened it down to stay. As I once saw in a newspaper advertisement, "it is as solid as an Insurance Company." Perhaps I have the words twisted, anyhow it is in a good place, and I advise governments to let it alone. We got back to the ship, after the highwaymen and palace-car porters had gone through us to their heart's content, sailing away at noon. We expect to reach Genoa, Thursday, about 5 P. M.

My journal continues:

JUNE 3rd, *Wednesday.*—"Two weeks from home to-day .... beautiful weather .... the Mediterranean as smooth as glass .... Captain's dinner this evening. Dancing on deck after."

The sail over the Mediterranean was the most enjoyable of our voyage as far as picturesqueness was concerned. At our right we could discern the dim outline of the African coast. Beyond, we passed along the border of the Riviera, Nice, Monte-Carlo, old Roman towers, the Balearic Islands, all an ever-changing landscape. The Mediterranean when behaving itself is a most beautiful piece of water. Its color, reflected from the pure Italian skies, is of the most intense blue, as if indigo had dyed it in every portion. It is said that when aroused, it can give points to the Atlantic. We prefer to leave the question unsettled.

The Captain's dinner given the evening before reaching the end of the voyage, is supposed to be a gorgeous affair. We saw no marked difference from those of other days. To be sure, there were a few more flags, some flowers and strawberries purchased at Gibraltar, but the "extras" cost the same, and the menu card was no longer, nor more varied. As our crowd was to separate, never to meet again here, or hereafter, so far as we knew, we ordered a full line of "antitoxine" and drank to each other's health and prosperity. I could do the former unselfishly as I was at the time out of the practice of medicine. The ball followed. As I laid myself down to sleep that night thinking of all that had been in the joyous days of the past two weeks, of what might come to us and to ours in the future, I could not help repeating:

> Oh joyous days, thy memory lingers,
> Like some sweet dream ye haunt me as we part:
> I'll close thy tomb with holy, tender fingers,
> Thou'lt lie embalmed 'mid spices of the heart.

We reached Genoa, Thursday, June 4th, at 6 o'clock, P. M.

It was a beautiful sight as we approached "La Superba." The sun shone full upon the city of palaces and reflected back the beams from off the blue waters at its feet. Nearer and nearer we drew. Not like the baseless fabric of a dream was it, but like a silver picture in a frame of gold. We were anxious to get ashore, though we sorrowed to leave behind those who had grown to be friends. At last the wharf was reached; the plank thrown out, and the medical officer of the Port stepped aboard. There was a long consultation with our doctor. We did not know what it meant. Perhaps there had been sickness in the steerage. Finally the parley came to an end and we were told to land.

I am addicted to a few small vices, the greatest

of which is an inordinate love for tobacco in the form of smoking. I use it only three times a day. My wife will bear me out in this, only she says I smoke from breakfast till dinner, from dinner till supper and from supper till I go to bed.

Among my effects purchased for the tour were a pipe and a reasonable supply of the weed. During the many conversations held in the smoke-room, I learned tobacco was under the ban of the Italian Goverment, and that I should be obliged to pay duty on what I had in stock as the amount held by me was beyond the lawful allowance. Now as I did not care to be arrested as an outlaw on my first appearance in this land of Saints, I talked the matter over with the first engineer, who told me to throw the stuff overboard and not try "to do" the Customs. I did not know so much as I do now, or I would have kept it. To act on his advice I thought a wicked waste, so asked him to accept it, which he did quite willingly. I can now see through his game.

We bade farewell to each fellow-passenger, including the smoke-room steward, several times. This latter hoped to meet us again. He really evinced more sorrow than some others with whom we had been more intimate. We gave him some marks and our pax. On leaving the ship after an ocean voyage the proper thing to do is to pay everybody something, no matter whether they have earned it or deserve it, or not. If you do not do it voluntarily they will suggest it. Also tell them what a good time you have had. Don't mind a little lying, they won't know and you won't care. Your room steward and stewardess really deserve a "pour boir," and so does the deck steward. If you have any money left after doing the right thing all around, give it to the captain. No one will be insulted, no one will refuse. It is a habit they have all over Europe, and you may just as well get into practice first as last. I'd take something myself after last year's experience.

When our luggage had been placed in care of the Custom House officers, we disembarked. We were met at the land end of the gang-plank by an interpreter whom we had engaged by cable. I gave him something as a starter. He knowing the ropes better than we, our trunk and bags were soon gone over, by the help of another remembrance quietly placed in the hand of the Inspector, and after being stamped were put into a carriage and with our personal remains in attendance taken to the hotel.

CHAPTER V.

GENOA.

*"Thy wreck a glory, and thy ruin graced
With an immaculate charm which cannot be defaced."*

GENOA, once called "*The Superb*," is now a back number and out of the business. Though still the chief commercial port of Italy, there are many cities in the New World which could give it points as far as "the superb" is concerned. Once when its palaces held dukes and duchesses, when fair women and brave men lived within the now ruined Palazzi, when history was being made, Genoa had a seat way up in front. I do not mean to say it is not of interest now. It is full of story and of remembrance. Take your Baedeker, (God bless him) and read up. Then buy a ticket and go to see it. It will cancel the expenditure. I will tell you how it appeared to us.

We reached the hotel (Londres) after a ride of about ten minutes. They have no tape-measures in Europe with which to measure distances. You go so long. I suppose when they lay out a railroad they bargain, or contract according to the time it takes to build it. We registered and went to our rooms. The sensations produced by walking about were singular ones. My legs felt as if they had rights of their own and wished to exercise them. I staggered as I presume men do when intoxicated. I know it was lost motion, lost land motion, lost on the ship and that I had not recovered my terrestrial equilibrium. Mary thought it might be due to the grief expressed, or absorbed, at saying good bye to the boys. I came out all right the next day.

After "regulating" things and opening that trunk, we fixed up a trifle. I thought I would stroll about the town, getting in as much of sight-seeing as possible, time being short and we getting near to our letter of credit. I went into the hall and rung for the elevator, supposing the cars ran as in hotels I am accustomed to patronize. After waiting half an hour, I walked down stairs to see what had become of the machine. I was informed what we in civilized countries call "elevators" are here, (and all over Europe, with few exceptions,) known as "lifts," that is, they take—lift you up, but you go down on your own merits. My wife experiences more difficulty in going down than in mounting stairways; this was therefore an unpleasant outlook. I found the ship's methods availed on land and soon had a satisfactory understanding with the engineer, the satisfaction costing about five lira—one dollar.

European elevators, or lifts, are not dangerous. They are however made of poor material and unable to stand any great strain. Mary broke every one in every hotel we visited. She says it was simply a coincidence; I know it was fact. If you desire an afternoon ride, get into one and tell whoever works the lever you wish to get out at the second story, what they call their second .... Start soon after luncheon and you may get up in time for dinner. Slow? Molasses in winter has a railroad speed compared to them. Their style differs in different hotels. This you will be thankful for. Some have a boy, (hired because he knows absolutely nothing about running the concern), to drive the hearse, and to let you out when you appear tired, or think you are somewhere in the neighborhood of your hall. Others are said to be "automatic." They are. You enter and tell the agent the name of the station at which you desire to stop. The door is shut, something is fixed, and you are let "go Gallagher." If you have led a decent life in this world, the chances are the funeral will stop at the proper place. We never went beyond.

The sights in the streets interested me greatly, everything was so novel. What looked like tramcars ran about apparently as the judgment of the horses dictated, there being no rails that I could see. They got along as well as if nickel-plate had been laid, the pavements were so smooth. You pay two centimes a ride and get a ticket included, that the conductor may know you are on the train. They never take it up, and I brought mine home so as to have them on hand when I go again. The streets, now and then, have sidewalks, except where they are extremely narrow. By narrow I mean three feet or less in width. Here and there you see a pair of stairs, leading from one street to another, up hill. It saves going around the block. The Police are the most gorgeous mortals I ever met. After I had seen a few dozens of them, I concluded the Italian army was encamped near by and the Major Generals were taking a a brief respite from duty by strolling through the town. They wear cocked hats, epaulets, buttons galore, and what appear to be gold swords dangling between their legs. The size of the weapon is somewhat larger than our cavalry sabre, and of the same shape. On top of all this is enough ornamentation to make them a first-class sign for a wholesale clothing establishment. I never saw them arrest anyone, though it appeared to me they had abundant opportunities. Wages must be low, or it does not pay to over-work themselves. While walking about and drinking in the kaleidoscopic views, I began to feel like taking a smoke. All my tobacco had gone, as I have stated, to the engineer aboard of the boat, so I purchased some cigars, (that is what they called them,) three of them, at a little shop presided over by a Seigniora, no doubt the wife of a Duke. They were alleged to be made of real Virginia leaf. If they were, I hope Italy has a monopoly of the crop. I've been in Virginia, but have never seen any tobacco that could, or would, hold a candle to this compound. These vanilla beans called cigars, are about eight inches long, three-quarters of an inch thick and black as a lead pencil. One end has a piece of straw glued on for a mouth-piece, or holder, and through the entire length runs a broom corn which you pull out before lighting, so as to get a draught and form the chimney. I smoked nearly a quarter of an inch of this insulated electric wire and threw the other two away. Then I bought cigarettes, on which I lived till reaching Amsterdam, where really goods cigars may be obtained. We dined at five o clock everything on the table being well cooked and served. Ice-water was the only dish lacking. My wife ordered a glass. The head waiter, evidently astounded at her rashness, sent for the Coroner and summoned a jury. I thought he did, as he was so long getting it. Perhaps they had to freeze it, or send into the Alps for a supply. When I am in Italy I do as the Italians do. I stick to Chianti, it's cheaper. Ice-water at twelve cents a glass and wine at six a litre make me prefer wine. It has always been necessary for me to practice economy, as my charges are low and my paying patients few.

In the evening we were visited by some of the ladies who had been fellow-passengers on the "Werra," the doctor, and the "Lunatic," who suggested visiting a place of amusement. Though I thought I had been in one ever since I put my feet on land, my wife and I accepted. I have not the faintest idea where we went. We followed the doctor, who seemed to know the city by heart. And why should he not? He had been here often enough. He took care of the "Belle of the ship," a young lady from Kentucky, who apparently had captured his heart for the time, or trip; the "Lunatic" guided my wife, (and he had his hands full) buying her flowers and paying other little attentions that did not make me at all jealous. I brought up the rear, now and then catching up with the procession to see that proper decorum was maintained. We landed in a Garden, where, to the disgust of my wife and the other ladies, bier, wine and smoke, make up the entertainment. My wife, as if to set an example of temperance, or assume a virtue, called for a lemonade. She got what she deserved, namely a bottle of what we know as lemon soda. She has learned to ask for "lemon squash" when she wants the real article. We returned late in the evening and walked up stairs. The "lift" was asleep. We again "arranged" things, and after lighting the two tallow dips, (extra charge) went to bed. Whatever may be said against the Italians, I'll stick up for their beds. I think the one I slept in was the most delicious, heavenly lay-out I have ever experienced. My wife said they were no better than those we had at home, but that we enjoyed and appreciated them more on account of the difference between them and the ship's berths. On the whole, I think her diagnosis was correct.

The next morning we went to breakfast by way of the "lift." That finished, we held a consultation as to our future route and sundry other matters, wrote letters, packed our steamer rugs and clothing to be sent to Liverpool, to await our sailing by the "Majestic" on August 12th. We here instituted a plan of sight-seeing which we found so convenient we continued it during our entire outing. First, we engaged a guide—in this case we took our Interpreter, hired a cab and told the duke on the box to drive to everywhere in the city, no matter how much time it consumed, or how many lira it cost. They have a curious way of urging on the horses. This is done, not by saying "get up" in Italian, but by a sort of chirrup, which it is impossible to express in words. It has the effect. Mary got it to perfection, and whenever she wished me to step lively made the whistling sound. In this way we saw the people, the buildings, the linen of the dukes and duchesses hanging out of the windows to dry, and every other outside thing in the place. After that we did interiors, museums, churches, palaces. It costs more than to follow "Baedeker," but the results are better and you get over the ground faster. We visited everything worth seeing, including the monument of Columbus, in the center of the spacious Piazza Aqua Verde, just around the corner from our hotel, a magnificent work of art, erected in 1862. The Cathedral, all the churches, of which the "Annunziata" is the most sumptuous; the white and red palaces; the house at 37 Vicco Dritto Ponticelo St., where Columbus was born in 1446; the Municipio, or town hall, where among many other objects of great interest I saw the violin of Paganini, locked in an iron vault, lined with quilted blue silk. The instrument is a "Guernarius." The fiddle of Savori lies beneath it. Both are taken out three times a year, played upon and put in order. They are priceless relics to him who knows anything of the mysteries of the king of instruments.

A volume could be written, filled with descriptions of what we saw this day. To guide-books and other histories of Italian cities I must refer the reader. I do not want to bring too many chestnuts into this. One place I must mention, the "Campo Santo," or burial ground, the most magnificent in the world. Perhaps we were attracted to it by reason of my association with the work laid out in it. Statuary most graceful and artistic, works of art in themselves, and worthy of a more noble resting place, line the long corridors for miles. Every nook, corner and space is adorned with them. Beneath your feet are the resting places of the dead, over which you walk, these wonderful monuments, mementoes of love and affection, bringing to mind heroic virtues, if the dead in life were in keeping with the grandeur of their tomb-stones. The whole is beyond description, and a more nimble pen than mine is needed to describe the magnificence of the spot. Italian art is a big thing. I've learned something about it and admire it. Prof. A. Springer, has written a good deal on the subject and to his exhaustive works I refer you. We had a great day of it and filled but not satiated, we returned to the hotel for dinner. In the evening I went to the theater. Mary was exhausted, so I allowed her to remain at home. The doctor, the "Lunatic" and I made up the crowd and filled the auditorium. It rained in torrents after the performance, and we walked to our domicile in the drenching outpour. The cars and omnibuses do not run at night. The wheels are tired. As I lay on my bed courting sleep, through my window came the sound of voices. Young fellows going home, or out for some lark, singing as only Italians can, now in soli, now in duetto, then in unison. It was a free concert occurring every few minutes as the young lads sauntered along. It would cost a dollar and a half in New York to hear singing that could not compare with this.

From Genoa many delightful excursions may be made. Our time being so limited we postponed falling into temptation until our next visit.

We bade farewell to the doctor, and to the "Lunatic," also to others of our boat friends who had remained with us during our stay in Genoa. There was a Professor of Astronomy, with his sister, a most charming girl who had come over with us, and were on their way to the North Cape to make some kind of observation on an eclipse of the sun. They had a good deal of trouble in getting there, and after all the pains taken the day was cloudy, and they did not see the display. They traveled with us as far as Florence, but from the day of leaving us at that point, we have not seen them. I'd like to meet the sister again. As for the Professor, I'll turn him over to my wife. We left for Pisa and Rome the next day.

CHAPTER VI.

PISA.

WE left Genoa for Rome via Pisa, June 6th, at 12:42 P. M. The railroad wends its way along the shores of the Mediterranean, through two hundred and fifty tunnels. I do not think this is exaggerated by one tunnel. The ride was one of surpassing interest, as every moment "new novelties" greeted the sight. Here and there vineyards, the vines hanging from the mulberry trees, festooned in every conceivable and fantastic shape. Olive groves and gardens, flowers blooming in almost tropic luxuriance. Men and women working in the fields, the women doing the hardest part of the labor, as they should. Once I saw a woman and a cow hitched to a plow, pulling it along as if it were a matter of course. The huts, or houses, built of stone, usually a single story high, are vine-clad, nestling amid flowers and blooms. Some ape great dignity, the stucco front ornamented between the stones with painted balconies making them appear as real. The roofs are covered with tiles, like a red drain pipe cut in two and placed side by side till the top of the building is covered. Where these fail to perform their function, straw or dried grass make up what is lacking. Horses are few and far between, the little donkey or jackass doing what horses do for us. It appears wonderful what these little animals accomplish, the loads they pull and the gait they keep up. To be sure the roads are like a floor, hard as stone can make them, without mud, holes or roughness. The carts are immense structures, with two wheels only, each nearly five feet in diameter, the thills big enough to be floor timbers and the entire get up cumbersome and crude. Still these little fellows draw them along at a good pace, even when laden so as to appear top-heavy. Once I saw four persons, two women and two men, attempt to mount one of these carts, though it seemed to be loaded sufficiently at the time. The last to mount was a stout woman. She got on by the rear and the weight of her anatomical structure so displaced the center of gravity, the poor little beast was lifted entirely from his feet and hung dangling in the air. The matter was adjusted after the aforesaid woman got off, and stowed her body nearer the middle of the ark. The harness is heavy enough for a derrick, the saddle the most ponderous of all the connections. It appears to me there is room in Italy for a chapter of the "Society for the Prevention of Cruelty to Animals." But you can't tell, the jackass may not be getting anything more than he deserves.

It was our first ride in a foreign railroad train.

We had heard much of the discomfort of travel by railroads in Europe, but I have failed to see it. I think it depends a good deal on the traveler. The cars are short, not much if any longer than twenty feet, with two wheels at each end, four in all. The car is divided into compartments of different classes. Some are entirely of the first-class, some of the second, some of the third. Then you find first and second mixed, then second and third. In Germany they have a fourth class, which may be used for military service in carrying troops and horses and such impedimenta. In our travels we used first-class in Italy and France, second in Germany, England and elsewhere. We did not try the fourth class, as in them you stand up. This division is good enough for any one unless he is a fool, or a Crœsus. We never traveled at night, so I can say nothing of the "sleepers." The ordinary compartments, I believe, are turned into them by pushing up the arms and giving you some bedding. I am not sure but you have to furnish the latter yourself. In England "Wagners" and "Pullmans" are being rapidly introduced. I saw no freight cars, that is box cars similar to ours. All the freight is placed on platforms and covered with tarpaulins, held down by ropes tied at the corners. There may be other varieties, but I do not remember them. The engines are small affairs, but powerful, very different in appearance to those we use. Some have cabs, others not. All the coaches are lighted by gas, and in Italy they are kept constantly burning as the number of tunnels is so great. A signal is placed in the top of each compartment with instructions how to use it if any danger threatens the train or passenger. The penalty for monkeying with it is severe. Little difference is seen in the make-up of the first and second class compartments. The former are perhaps a trifle more luxuriously furnished, and have a looking glass. The glass seems to be the principal ornamentation, even when the seats are covered with velvet plush, as they usually are. The leather-covered ones in the second class are much cooler and more agreeable. Overhead are large and capacious racks for holding rugs, umbrellas, bundles and purchases. Beneath the seats is ample room to stow away the baby, and other useless articles. The motion of the carriage while running is an oscillating one, very disagreeable to those who suffer from the impediment of adipose, not unpleasant to the average weight. It bothered Mary somewhat. In all the trains we had every comfort, lavatories, observation platforms, towels, drinking water, every convenience of travel. The seats are across, not length-wise of the compartment. There are two in each, facing. Each is divided by a movable arm, which may be turned up at night, or at any time. The seats hold eight persons. In some compartments smoking is allowed, in others not, there being no special "smoker." In those in which it is permitted, ash-receivers and other conveniences are at hand for the user of the weed. Above each seat is a map of the route and full explanations of the rules of the company in four languages, Italian, German, French and English. Ten or twelve of these cars usually make up a train. They do not run on "Empire Express" time, the average for the fastest being about twenty-five miles an hour. This, I judge, is done in order that the people may think they have a large country, for should the speed be much faster than it is, the whole business would shoot out of the domain in an hour or two, thus producing unbelief in their geographies, or start a revolution. The road-beds are magnificent, far ahead of those in America. Stone fences separate them from the highways and adjoining lands, the sides being walled up making them smooth and clean in appearance. "Grade crossings" go under the track, so the train and the country wagons do not occupy the same space at the same time. The experiments made in my native land to accomplish this feat have proved disastrous to all but surgeons. The coal used is pressed into blocks about three times the size of an American brick. It is smooth and polished like marble. At every station it is piled in immense stacks ready for loading upon the tender.

The starting of a train is no small affair. It is a regular Fourth of July. It is not done by the stroke of a bell, or the wave of a hand. Oh, no! We do it in that way, they don't. It is too big a thing, too big a business to be let off in so unostentatious a manner. It merits more attention. First a horn is blown; then the station-bell is rung; then the conductor has his innings and blows another horn; last the engineer whistles and the train moves on. The whistle on the locomotive is, from its sound, about an inch long and one-quarter of an inch in diameter. It makes no more noise than the willow variety constructed by the average school boy, not so much. I never passed another train in motion. One stands still, till the other has gone on. This insures safety. The tracks are, as a rule, single ones, but have more curves than a work on Geometry. The station houses are large and divided into departments, or offices, as numerous as a lottery agency. Telegraph wires are strung along the road and that they may not get out of order, or fall down, two poles, often three, hold the wire at the same point. This is too frequent to be an accident, it is the rule. Block-signals are coming into use, but how operated I know not. I saw no towers, hence think they are worked by a string.

This is about the way you board a train: First give some money to everybody in the hotel, including the cook, whom you probably have never seen. Then hire a carriage. Pay the porter for putting your trunks and other traps on board, after giving something to the hall-man for strapping them and bring them down stairs. Ride to the station. Pay the driver his fare, and remunerate him for the honor he has conferred upon you in permitting you to ride in his vehicle. A man now meets you as you dismount to take your hand-luggage. Pay him something for his act of kindness. Another takes your trunks into the baggage-room. Don't forget him, or he will jog your memory. Then buy your ticket. You give the agent his present when you buy it, it is included in the charge. Have your trunks and kit weighed. This will cost a coin of the realm for the trouble. You are then handed a piece of paper, with some unintelligible jargon and figures on it, a duplicate of which is pasted on your trunk for identification. This they think is "checking." They do it this way because they know no better. It serves its purpose, however, and as a rule, you get what you pay for—that is, your trunks. You think you are done paying. Oh, no. You have only struck the preface. At the door of the platform is another angel to help you and your flowers, umbrellas, luncheon and such, into your compartment. He has a large family in destitute circumstances, and as you do not wish to go out of the country knowing you have left a suffering mortal behind, when it is in your power to help him out of the scrape, present him with a tip. After you are in your seat you count your change, and look over your letter of credit to see if you have enough to get a night's lodging. Soon they yell out something which I presume may be translated "all aboard," the guard shuts and fastens the door, and after the concert of bells, trumpets and whistles by the officials is over, the train starts. I could not do the thing better myself.

I have heard a good deal said about being "locked in" these compartments. For the life of me I cannot see why a man in his senses wants to get out while the train is in motion. Mary nor I did not. The statement is over drawn. You are no more "locked in" than you are in our own cars. If you wish to open the door you may do so, and you may take a walk on the little platform running around the car. It is against the rules, but you take your chances. The door is kept shut for your safety. If you want to break your neck, it is not the company's fault. Another good thing about these railroads is, you cannot, unless you are a blank fool, get into the wrong train, or out at the wrong station. This is the mode of procedure: Buy a ticket. It is then looked at by a man at the gate, then by another, after you have passed the turnstile: then before you get into the car, then before the train starts, and last by the guard before the funeral has gone so far the corpse cannot get home by walking. The process is reversed when you arrive at where you wish to stop. The guards on the train, one to each car, take the places of our conductors. (Don't forget to give him something in the way of money before you get off.) They have a seat on the top of the trap, where they look out and study the country, every now and then coming down to see if you are on board. They are polite, when you can make them understand what you are talking about, or are going to give them something. They are all uniformed, and don't bother you looking at your ticket every ten minutes. At each important station the doors of the compartments are thrown open and you may take a stroll about the town before the train leaves if you so desire. At every place where the train stops if only for a minute, wine, sausages, sandwiches, fruit and other edibles are offered for sale by boys or women. Water is difficult to obtain. Everything sold is reasonable (comparatively,) clean and good. At a starting station when the train has a long run, as from Paris to Calais, lunch-baskets may be bought, and for a dollar you get a bottle of wine, a chicken, rolls and butter, knife and fork, napkins, tumbler, and some fruit. It is sufficient for one and often for two. The basket which contained the viands is left in the compartment and gets back to the owner—somehow. When you land at your desired haven you begin paying out the same as when you started, simply reversing the motion. The same band of robbers is around and not one of the gang is missing. You get tired after you have been doing it all the time for three months. The gratuities however are small. We soon got into the habit of filling our pockets with what Mary called "chicken feed," and a couple of dollars would last us a day or longer, if we kept our heads and did not mistake francs for centimes. Never hesitate about giving, no matter how small the amount. It will always be acceptable either in a church, saloon, museum or catacomb. You'll be made uncomfortable if you do not. The only thing to remember is, not to give too much. If you do, you will have more attention from the natives than I usually bestow on my wife. The reader is beginning to ask what all this talk has to with Pisa. I answer, nothing. It is only a means to an end.

PISA is a quiet town, the capital of a province and situated six miles from the sea on both banks of the Arno, over which one may cross by either of four bridges. It became a Roman colony one hundred and eighty years B. C., and looks as if it had not recovered from it yet. The biggest thing in it is the "Piazza Duomo," where are located the Leaning Tower, Cathedral, the Baptistery and the Campo Santo. To this every one goes as soon as he sets foot in the place. The Cathedral, Leaning Tower, the Baptistery with the Campo Santo, form a group which, like Barnum's show, has no equal of its kind on earth. It is outside the city proper, and they keep the Tower there for fear it may tumble over on some of the boys going home late at night. In the Cathedral is the bronze lamp from the swaying of which Galileo got the idea of grandfather's clock. The idea was a good one as long as it lasted. The interior is like all other cathedrals, filled with altars, candles, pictures and wooden saints, images of the originals and just as good. The Baptistery is a kind of annex to the cathedral and is run by the Baptist end of the Roman church. It was started in 1153 and does not yet appear completed The eight-story Clock Tower, called "The Leaning Tower," thirteen feet out of plumb in a height of 179 feet, is surrounded by a lot of columns to hold it up. These run to the top, practically making the whole machine. Some one was off his base when it was started, or full, which has produced the curious effect that has given it so much distinction. Temperance people say the leaning is due to the settling of the foundations. You may take your choice. I have my opinion. Galileo worked up a lot of business for Gravitation by reason of this crookedness, and helped Physics to be more stupid than its forefathers intended. This tower has seven bells, four more than a church near my residence at home. I pity the people. Those at home are rung every Sunday morning at 7:30. Now there are only about half a dozen Christians within sound of the noise, all others in the neighborhood being otherwise. I never could understand the need of cutting up the row they do, just for the sake of getting so few inside the Insurance building at so early an hour. They pay their bills no quicker during the week. I am opposed to bells, not only on the score of disturbance to health, but because I own a watch. The Campo Santo is built out of fifty-three ship-loads of earth brought from Mount Calvary. They freighted the land over at reduced rates, so those who thought themselves better than common folks might lie snugger than the other bugger buried elsewhere. Every one planted in it is as dead as a smelt, and their foreign address is unknown. I do not see that they can rise any sooner than if they had been cremated. It is every one to his taste. Mary says when she dies she wants to go to Paris, not to Pisa. All the buildings contain paintings and frescoes, more or less poor. Some are said to be good. I am no judge. At any rate they have age with them.

Beside these unusual attractions, there is a University and any number of common churches, all owned by a Saint syndicate; at least they are named after some one of the lot. It's a large company. From what I have seen I should think there were nearly half a million in Italy alone, that is Saints. The Lungarno is the busy part of the city, where are the wharves extending along both banks of the river. If you wish to know all we saw in Pisa, get your Baedeker and read up. The print is fine and so are the descriptions.

CHAPTER VII.

ROME.

"The Niobe of Nations."

WE reached the Eternal City at 11:30 P. M. and were driven to the Hotel Minerva. It is near the center of the city, on the Piazza della Minerva, beside the church of S. Maria Minerva and within sight of the Pantheon. Before it stands a monument made up of an elephant in marble, on the back of which a small ancient obelisk was placed by Bernini in 1667. We slept well after our long ride and awoke early. Here, as elsewhere, everything is left-handed. The correspondence paper has its name and announcement on the last page. You dry your writing with sand instead of with blotting pads; doors open in, when they should open out, and have locks and keys large enough for a state prison. The floors are of stone, covered with rugs, or pieces of carpet. Candles try to dispel the darkness at night, after the twilight which lingers here till near midnight is done.

"The lifts" are the same freight and accommodation trains as in all European hotels. No one need hesitate about traveling in Italy, or, in fact, any country of Europe, by reason of a want of knowledge of the country's language. English is spoken everywhere, at the hotels, at the tourist agencies, by the guides and by many you meet in the streets and stores. If any foreign tongue is to be acquired, let it be French. With this latter you can get along without the slightest trouble. Nearly everyone speaks it, especially in Italy, from the shoe-black on the street to the driver on the hack. I bought a "Phrase book" before leaving home, warranted to contain all useful (?) expressions in four languages. It was a snare and a delusion. Listen to this as an example: "Bring me your carriage and horses, that I may see them, and if I like them I will buy them." Did you ever read anything more idiotic? What I wanted to say was: "Bring me some more bier," or something that was like it, matters that pertained to my temporal and spiritual welfare. Real solid experiences are not in these "horn books." Then there are no swear-words. I never use profanity, but I often think it, especially when traveling. You can't get along without it. If you can swear in a foreign language it eases you up, and don't count against you later, that is in the "sweet bye and bye." You think swear so often in Europe when you are called upon to pay for what you have not had, that it pays to have it on tap, and always proves itself a good thing. You feel better when the depth of the circumstances de mands it. A friend of mine wrote me out a lot of words, but forgot to put the "swear" in. They were of no earthly use. He is a Presbyterian. I caught onto a few gems, more or less forcible, from the guide, and I use them even now. I can swear at Mary and she thinks I am calling her pet names. She swears, but her methods differ from mine. I understand her.

It is impossible to describe in words how Rome impressed us. One must see it. Only then will he know how it feels. You cannot *tell* it, you *feel* it. As you walk through the city your history and your classics come back. You dream of the centuries long gone when Rome was mistress of the world. You walk under triumphal arches, enter the Pantheon, the only ancient edifice which is still in perfect preservation, visit the houses of the Cæsars, go down into the prison where Paul and Peter were confined, stand within the churches and beside the tombs, upon the places where men have died "without the shedding of blood" for what was then called heresy, and what we know now as truth. You see in mental vision, the wild beasts in the dens of the Colosseum, the victim waiting in the arena; the Emperor, the Vestal Virgins, and the populace filling the auditorium: you hear the applause, or see the thumbs turned down. What memories rise, what shudders creep over you! You love it, yet hate it. Here learning was advanced, but freedom of thought and science were throttled. Here was the center of the world, and here men died that Truth might live.

As "Rome was not built in a day," so its wonders cannot be seen in a hasty visit. A year is all too short to grasp, or even read the preface of the interesting volume here opened. From the Dome of Saint Peter's, and the tomb of Hadrian, across the Bridge of the Cæsars, to the end of the Appian Way, by the Mausoleums of those who have carved out the history of the world, each spot, each stone, every vista calls to mind some incident fraught with memories. To the Christian, and to the Unbeliever, Rome has its pages written in records that defy the tooth of Time. All that is beautiful in art is here. The brush of the painter, and the chisel of the sculptor adorn corridor and aisle. Temples and palaces tell of the might and power of church and state; Pope, prince and potentate speak of rule and influence, reaching out to the ends of the earth. How unspeakably grand it is, how dwarfed one feels amid these records of the past and present.

Sunday was our first day in this marvelous place. We engaged a guide at once, and he proved the best in all our journeyings. He had been the escort of many distinguished Americans, and had honored them by accepting their cards, to which collection I added mine, after paying him five liras a day and giving him some money as a remembrance. I shall try to get hold of him on my next visit.

We went first to the Forum, through the ruins of the Ancient City to the Colosseum, spending many hours among these reminders of years long gone. We went, however, to vespers at St. Peter's in the afternoon, so got credit for being religious. The King broke the day by reviewing the troops and having a grand display of fireworks in the evening.

We saw many of the Italian soldiers just returned from Africa, and a sorry lot they were, from the thrashing they received. Each day we visited the hitherto unknown and dreamed of places of interest. St. Peter's, the churches, the vatican, monuments, arches and ways, statues and columns, galleries and paintings, fountains and baths, catacombs and tombs, gardens and shops, temples and prisons ; saw dead Popes and live ones, saints and sinners, fat and jolly Cardinals and Bishops, and the barefooted missionary, types of every order belonging to the great church ; crossed the Tiber again and again, saw everything, in fact, that makes Rome the grandest and most historically interesting city in the world. To a pen like that of Gibbon must be left the description of them all : my poor diction feels its poverty of words. We visited the catacombs of Callistus, on the Via Appia, the most interesting of all the catacombs in Rome. Less fantastic than that of the "Capuchins," they have the merit of being older, and contain more of what is left of genuine saints. I tried to obtain of the custodian a small relic in the shape of a bone, but he refused to part with any, though his stock was large. I offered to buy one at his own price. Strange to say, this met with a refusal. As a last resort I offered to turn Catholic and allow him to baptize me then and there. I got no bone. Perhaps I did not know the ropes. In my business a toe-joint would have been a big advertisement, as I might have announced miracles could be worked on the sick during office-hours at the old price. An increase in the number of patients was looked for to make the investment pay. I brought home the remains of the little candle I used in my investigation of the tombs. There may be some virtue in that.

The Piazza Campo di Fiore, was to me a spot fraught with sadness and thought, for here on Feb. 17th, 1600, the hero, Giordano Bruno, suffered death by being burned at the stake; his heresy, the assertion that there were other worlds than ours. Where that noble life went out, on the spot where stood the stake, now stands a monument. Upon its top a statue. It is that of Bruno, and the inscription reads "Sanctus Bruno." The dome of St Peter's, and the columns of the Vatican are just beyond. Some of us who are heretics to-day may be saints to-morrow. Who knows? The world moves.

In Rome carriage hire is cheap. For the equivalent of a dollar, we had a "Fiacre" with a driver the entire day. This wage does not include your present, which if you feel particularly generous, may amount to ten cents, half a lira. You can get around by the tram-cars if you wish to save money, or reduce expenses, but it is less annoying by the carriage, beside saving much walking. The exchange on my gold paid all this, and left something over for lemon squashes for Mary. The water in Rome is pure and plentiful. Ice is scarce. The old aqueduct of Claudius is still used in part and the supply is full and abundant. Fountains play everywhere, and the stream is not the size of a goose quill either. It rushes in torrents, cooling all about it. We had been told not to go so far south at this time of the year, as Roman fever was apt to find lodgement in the unacclimated. We took the chances and quinine. I think all this talk about Roman fever is largely exaggerated. Medical and Sanitary Science have done much to abort it by better drainage, drying the low lands, as in the Compagnia, and furnishing a more abundant supply of wholesome water. That it does occur I do not doubt, especially in the fall months. Winter is really the time to visit the city. The only thing I should fear being the inability to keep warm. The modes of heating seem very primitive and not likely to accomplish the desired result. The stoves, (there is no hot-air or steam heat that I saw) are high porcelain boxes with the feed-door and all means of regulating them out in the hall, beyond the reach of him who desires to keep warm. Your comfort depends evidently on the friendly relations you establish with the hall-boy. I suppose you get so much caloric for so many soldi.

The Romans are great rascals as tradesmen. I have not met "the noblest of them all." They catch on to you as soon as they see you, and knowing you are a foreigner put up the price. After a few days when I went shopping, I passed myself off as a Spaniard, (this was before the war) hoping to get rates somewhere near the value of things. I do not know whether it made any difference or not.

As in all European cities, the inhabitants live out of doors when the weather and temperature permit. Little tables are seen everywhere in front of the cafés, and men and women taking luncheon, or drinking wine. They do not seem to be annoyed by flies, though fleas attract a good deal of attention. Ask Mary. We bought here, as elsewhere, photographs of all noted pictures and statuary, as well as of the most interesting ruins and buildings, sending them home unmounted by registered post, thereby saving the payment of duty. It is useless to say our stay was all too short. Weeks may be spent in investigating all that is here to be seen. A life-time could hardly complete it. Old, before Time began its overthrow, Rome is ever new. Each turn brings to view a lovelier historic picture. Its temples tell of its might and power; its ruins of what it has been. It would almost seem as if the prophetic saying of the pilgrims of the eighth century was true:

> "While stands the Colosseum, Rome shall stand,
> When falls the Colosseum, Rome shall fall,
> And when Rome falls, with it shall fall the world."

Of course many amusing incidents occurred during our stay. I recall one in particular. We had been "doing" the town in the morning, and had stopped at a cafè for luncheon. The guide excused himself, saying he wished to go home, as his wife was ill, but would return before we were ready to sally forth to new adventures. The Professor and his pretty sister were with us. After seating ourselves at the table, the menu was placed before us. It was written, or printed, in Italian, (we never could decide which) and in so poor and illegible a style, that even the Professor, with all his learning, could not decipher it. It looked like a sixth copy done on a third-hand type-writer. I think it was etched with a broken electric pen, or perhaps it was one of those "fountain" fellows. We tried to read it so as to make a selection, but did not order for fear of getting something we would not relish, or entirely different from what we supposed, as did a traveling acquaintance in Germany, who ordered what he supposed were strawberries, but got potatoes. We decided on macaroni, though we had eaten it in all the forms and disguises into which the Italians are capable of putting it. It came, and such a plate, or deckful. Mounted in tomatoes and other decorations, it was a beauty. My wife, as chaperon of the party, was requested to serve it. She had seen the natives tackle the job, and in her innocency thought she was as agile as they. She failed. How to get those long nursing tubes onto a plate was the trouble. In a fit of desperation she made hash of the lot and served it to us as best she could. We ate it, but not in due and ancient form. In trying to get the mess into our mouths, most of it went back to the plates, on the table, or floor. We earned by honest labor what we subsequently paid for in hard cash. It is an art to eat macaroni. The Italians have a knack of sticking a fork into the mass, rolling the fork over two or three times, when it goes into the mouth as slick as you please. No trouble whatever. We did not acquire the modus operandi. To my mind an easy way would be to throw it over a clothes line and eat upwards. It would not be æsthetic, but you'd get the macaroni.

It was here Mary began to get in full swing at an expression she had practiced on shipboard, namely, "Don't." The word was always aimed at me, I must own. All through our journey, when she could think of nothing else to say, she said "don't." She is not over the habit yet. If I had a centime for every time she hurled it at me, I'd be a man of wealth and could support all her relations. It was omnipresent in her conversations. If you could not understand the word, you'd think she was talking a streak in Italian, or French. I paid no attention to it after a while, because I could always tell when it was coming in, or should do so. It is a useless word, so far as I am concerned, and tends to stifle freedom of action or speech. Somehow I cannot break her of the habit. She never uses it when I offer her a ten dollar note. Strange, is it not?

I purchased a lot of beads in the Catacombs, said to have been blessed by the Holy Father, (they were by me several times before I reached home, but I used other formulæ than those prescribed by the Church.) I bought them as little remembrances to my truly apostolic patients. In order that they might be known as genuine, I had the monk put his "ne varietur" in the shape of a stamp on the lot. This cost a franc extra, and did the beads good. My only regret was that bone, and I shall never forgive the saint for his selfishness. Roman mosaics are sold in all the shops and by boys on the streets. All are dear in price. The Colosseum and St. Peter's are the favorite designs. In St. Peter's there are few pictures, the ornamentation other than the tombs of the Popes and Saints being the most exquisite copies in mosaic of the celebrated paintings and works of art in the Vatican galleries. We went through the factory, or studio of the Pope, where these magnificent copies are made. Some take a life-time in being put together, and are kept for the adornment of the great cathedral. Many are on sale, but the price of those I wanted was beyond my means, and my wife did not wish to forego a Paris bonnet in order to indulge my æsthetic tastes. On thing I must mention. The bronze statute of St. Peter. It is of the 5th century and stands near the principal entrance. It is an object of adoration by the devout. As they pass by in line, each gives the right foot a wipe with his sleeve to remove the microbes, then presses his lips to it, and goes on a better man (it is to be hoped). Mary would not do it. She says she prefers to kiss a real live man, and on the lips. She does not wish to waste her sweetness on brass. She's right. I myself prefer living Madonnas to oil paintings. By this frequent osculation kept up daily for so many centuries, the toes are worn away as far back as the ball of the foot. I wonder where they have gone. I honor all men who respect and live up to their religious views, but I draw the line at Peter's toes.

We left Rome at 8:20 A. M. arriving in Naples at 1:30 P. M. the same day.

CHAPTER VIII.

NAPLES. POMPEII.

"Vedi Napoli e poi mori."

NAPLES is noted for its beggars and fleas, and celebrated for its bay and museum. The beggars comprise every blessed man in the city. The fleas began on Mary in Genoa. They know a good thing when they see it. We arrived at 13:30 o'clock, which means 1:30 in the afternoon in civilized countries. After all, I do not know but this method of computing time is a good one, as you never get the morning A. M. mixed up with the afternoon P. M.

We found quarters at the Victoria Hotel on the banks of the bay. The Island of Capri with its blue and green grottoes was before us, the mountain of St. Elmo at our right, Vesuvius at our left. The bay is the most beautiful in the world, there is no question about it. The water blue as indigo, the landscape clothed in vines, here and there a sail, everything is a picture, all a dream.

After a good luncheon, we started out for a drive. We rode all over the city and up to the Convent of St. Martin, where we indulged in several samples of "Chartreuse." I liked it so well, I would have brought the machinery for making it home, had it not been for the Raines Law. Near the end of the Strada di Piedigrotta, which forms the Grotta Nuova di Posilipo, is the tomb of Virgil. The name of the monument is without satisfactory historical foundation, but probability and local tradition favor the presumption that it was Virgil's last resting place. I am glad I saw it. His assumed poetry made my life miserable in youth, and broke up many a game of ball. I have never used his Eclogues or Bucolics in my practice since I read them, so what good have they done me.

Beggars are everywhere. They follow your carriage, cluster about you when you shop, and are only a trifle more bold than the tradesmen. Fleas are thicker than hair on a dog. They stick to you like leeches. We brought specimens into England—in our wraps. The National Museum is one of the finest in the world, not surpassed by the British Museum in London. It started as a cavalry barrack in 1588. Since 1790 it has been fitted up for the reception of the royal collection of pictures and antiquities. Ferdinand 1st, in 1816, gave it the name of Muse Real Borbonico. Here are united the collections belonging to the crown, the Farnese collection from Rome and Parma, those of the Palaces of Portici and Capodimonte, and the excavated treasures of Herculaneum, Pompeii, Stabiæ and

Cumæ. This whole now forms one of the finest collections in the world. The Pompeian antiquities and objects of art in particular, as well as the bronzes from Herculaneum, are unrivalled. Within this museum is a "Sacred Room," to which gentlemen only are admitted. Modesty forbids describing it. I also saw here many surgical instruments taken from the buried city of Pompeii, which were to me of great professional interest; scalpels, forceps, specula and many other tools, much like our modern implements of medical and surgical warfare. Evidently the doctors of that date were in with the undertakers, as they are to-day.

After dark we would walk along the border of the bay, toward Mt. Vesuvius, watching the lava in blood-red streams running down the sides. It was a beautiful sight. During the day the smoke could be seen lazily rising from the several craters near the summit. The whole thing looked just as it did in my old geography. I remember the picture well, at the lower corner of the right hand page. I hoped then to see it. I have. Would that all the dreams of boyhood days might end as happily.

They have a queer way of doing business over here. When anything extraordinary is to take place, as a National Exhibition, Fair, Horse Trot, or an Eruption of Vesuvius, instead of trying to get a crowd to come by cutting down rates, carfares and reducing hotel prices, everything goes up double. They say it is their innings, and they intend to make hay while the sun shines. They are correct as far as their exchequer is concerned, but it's outings for the visitors. I think Mary enjoyed the view of the bay more than any scenery while abroad. She kept her eye on it day and night, so it would not get away. Also on me. I give her credit for fine taste. It was great. The weather now became much warmer, though the days were clear and we had no rain of any account, not enough to interfere with our pleasures.

Being so near to Pompeii, I decided to run over and take a look at what was left of it. By reason of the increased warmth, and as the whole journey over the buried city must be done on foot, Mary deemed it best to remain in Naples and allowed me to go with the Professor and his pretty sister. It was not long before I was gone with the sister and the Professor going alone. I was still unmarried and did not like to see so charming a girl neglected.

Before retiring the night prior to going to Pompeii, Mary and I held a caucus as to future movements. We decided to go home by way of Lombardy, Switzerland, Bavaria, Austria, Germany, Holland, Belgium, France and England, after looking into one or two places remaining in Italy. We bought a few rembrances for friends the following day and considered all contracts closed.

POMPEII.

POMPEII is very like a corpse at a funeral. The minister tells all about how good the dear departed has been, but says nothing of the remains in the front parlor. Leaving Naples at 8:20 in the morning, we reached the late lamented after a ride of an hour. As you step from the cars and follow the street, it reminds you of Coney Island. Booths, eating houses, ticket agents and souvenir peddlers, are at every point. We took luncheon, and after some discussion of the "whys and wherefores," decided not to ascend Vesuvius, as it was warm and the crust uncertain. Cook has a railway for about half the distance, the remaining ascent being made on foot, or on donkey back. It costs several dollars to do do it right, and you bring back nothing but tired legs, a strong smell of sulphur and the motto "I have been up." I could have told Mary that I had "been up" if the Professor and his sister had not been around, and she would have believed it, regarding me as a greater hero than ever. But I never lie, that is, except to Mary.

Pompeii is mentioned for the first time in history, B. C. 310. Its monuments, however, prove it of much greater antiquity. After many vicissitudes of war and earthquakes, it got knocked out in A. D. 63. It however revived, only to be overtaken by the final castrophe of August 24th, A. D. 79. Showers of ashes and rapilli from the burning mountain covered it to a depth of seven, or eight feet. The present superincumbent mass is about twenty feet in thickness, the result of subsequent eruptions. In 1748, the discovery of some statues and bronze utensils by a peasant, attracted the attention of Charles III, who caused excavations to be made. All this you can read in Baedeker, or other books. The town, if you call it one, has a museum and library supported by the goverment. Most of the moveable objects and frescoes have been removed to the museum at Naples; many, however, are left and are worth seeing. The museum here contains much of interest, though nothing of artistic value. There are amphoræ, vases, rainspouts, etc., in terra-cotta, vessels in bronze, carbonized articles of food, skulls and skeletons of men and animals. There are many interesting casts of bodies. Although the soft parts had decayed in course of time, their forms frequently remained imprinted on the ashes, which afterwards hardened. In 1863 Fiorelli, made the ingenious experiment of carefully removing the bones and filling the cavity with plaster, and he has succeeded in preserving the figures and attitudes of the deceased after their death-struggle. Among the figures are, a young girl with a ring on her finger, two women, one tall and elderly, the other younger. A man lying on his face, and one lying on his left side, with the features remarkably well preserved.

The town was built in the form of an irregular ellipse. The excavated portion embraces not quite half, but probably the most important part of it. It includes the Forum with the contiguous temples and public buildings, two theatres with large colonnades, the ampitheater and a considerable number of private dwellings more or less ornate. The streets, bordered by sidewalks, are straight and narrow, being paved with large polygonal blocks of lava. At intervals, especially at the corners, are placed high stepping stones intended for the convenience of foot passengers in rainy weather. The chariot wheels have left deep ruts where traffic was most frequent. At the corners are public fountains decorated with the head of a god, a phallus, a mask, or a similar ornament. Notices are frequently seen painted in red letters, referring to the election of the municipal officers, and recommending some particular individual as ædile, or duumvir. Stuccoed walls are often covered with roughly scratched drawings, resembling those with which our streets Arabs still delight to decorate blank surfaces. What have been the busiest streets may be identified by means of the shops, which were let to merchants in the same way as the ground floors of the Palazzi in Naples are occupied by the shops of the present day. These shops were generally in no way connected with the back part of the house, but presented their whole frontage to the street. Many of the shop tables, covered with marble, and not unfrequently fitted up with large earthen vessels for the sale of wine, oil, etc., are still preserved. The great number of these affords proof of the importance of the retail trade at Pompeii.

Where there are no shops, the streets are very monotonous. The absence of glass in the windows forms one of the chief differences between an ancient and a modern dwelling. The ancients concentrated their domestic life in the interiors, the houses presenting to the street a blank wall with as few openings as possible, and these covered with an iron grating. One of these gratings, the only one I think left, is still to be seen. It was in the second story. The dwelling houses vary greatly in size, and have obviously been very differently fitted up, in accordance with the nature of the situation, or the means and tastes of the owner. Most of the houses of the wealthy class are entered from the street by a narrow passage, which is surrounded by a covered one leading to the court, with the reservoir for rain-water in the center. The roof (I saw none) evidently sloped inwards for the purpose of admitting light and air to the court and adjoining rooms. On each side and sometimes in front were the bedrooms.

The front of the house was devoted to intercourse with the external world, and it was here the boss received his clients if a lawyer, his patients if a doctor, and the merchant transacted business. The center consisted of an open court or garden enclosed by columns. Around were situated the sleeping and dining-rooms, the rooms for the slaves, kitchen, cellar, &c. Most of the apartments were very small, the family working and spending their time in the light and airy courts. The wall decorations in Pompeii lend it a peculiar charm. Marble is rarely met with in domestic architecture, and not often in the public works, the columns being constructed of tuffstone, or bricks. These bricks, like all the bricks of the ancients, are about an inch thick, four inches wide and a foot long. The walls and columns were then covered with stucco and painted. The lower halves are generally red, or yellow, the capitals tastefully colored. The walls, where they are undecorated, are painted with bright and almost glaring colors, chiefly red and yellow, harmonizing with the brilliancy of the southern sun. The center of the walls is generally occupied by a painting unconnected with the others. The best have been removed to the Museum at Naples, to protect them from the exposure to the weather. The scenes present a soft, erotic character corresponding to the peaceful and pleasure-seeking taste of the age. I wished I had lived there.

CHAPTER IX.

FLORENCE.

"Thou art the garden of the world, the home of all Art yields."

WE always traveled on Sunday, when the rides were to be long; not that we were irreligious, (Mary is an Episcopalian, and I belong to all the churches, including the Masons, Odd Fellows, Knights of Pythias, Royal Arcanum and some others,) but because the entrance fee to all museums and galleries is abolished on that day, so the poorest may enjoy their priceless treasures. This gives rise to crowds, and is unpleasant when you wish solitude to gaze upon and think over relics and works of art. Another reason, it gave us Monday to ride about, as that was "cleaning day" after the crowd of visitors of the day before.

Leo has written an apotheosis of Florence, which it would ill become me to attempt to improve. He says: " .... Like a water lily, rising on the mirror of the lake, so rests this lovely ground, the still more lovely Florence, with its everlasting works, and its inexhaustible riches. From the bold, airy tower of the palace, rising like a slender mast, to Brunelleschi's wondrous dome of the Cathedral; from the old house of the Spini, to the Pitti palace, the most imposing the world has ever seen; from the garden of the Franciscan convent, to the beautiful environs of the Casine, all are full of incomparable grace. Each street of Florence contains a world of art: the walls of the city are the calyx containing the fairest flowers of the human mind—and this is but the richest gem in the diadem with which the Italian people have adorned the earth."

Dante Alighieri really made the place, by being born here in 1265. You will remember he wrote "The Divine Comedy" and founded the Italian language; this latter was the worst thing he did. Boccaccio boarded in it, and a lot of other notables in Florentine history. Among the most distinguished was the family of the Medici, whose brilliant court has never been equaled. The history of Florence and Florentine art is one of greatest interest, and should be studied by all who expect to go there, if not as a part of a liberal education. I cannot tell you all we saw. Read the following books, and you will know what Florence holds, gems that no other place on earth contains.

"Walks in Florence," by the Misses Horner. "Tuscan Cities" and "A Florentine Mosaic," by W. D. Howell's. Hare's "Florence." Ruskin's "Mornings in Florence." "Romola," by George Eliot. Mrs. Oliphant's "Makers of Florence." "Echoes of Old Florence," by Leader Scott. "The

First Two Centuries of Florence," by Professor Pasquale Villare, and last but not least, "Baedeker's Northern Italy."

The Chief attractions are the Piazza della Signoria, with the Palazzo Vecchio, where Savonarola was burned, May 23rd, 1498, and the Loggia dei Lanzi, the Galleria degli Uffizi, the Piazza dei Duomo, with the Cathedral and Campinile, the unrivalled work of Giotto, the Baptistery, and its "Gates of Paradise," the churches of Carmine, S. Cruce, in which are the tombs of Michael Angelo and Galileo; S. Lorenzo, S. Maria Novello, Annuziata, S. Spirito, the Monastery of St. Marco, where is the cell in which Savonarola lived. Then the Pitti Palace and the Boboli Gardens, the Academy and the National Museum, Dante's and Galileo's and Michael Angelo's homes, a thousand objects of interest, all ever new, all fraught with beauty and pleasure. Florence is a quarry, from which treasures may be dug such as the world will never see again. To write about, or mention one-tenth of all we saw, the beautiful frescoes, the paintings, handiworks of the greatest geniuses the world has produced, the stained glass in the windows of the grand cathedrals and churches, through which the Italian sun pours its beams with a celestial glory, statuary, the buildings, the everything that makes Florence what it is, would, it seems to me, take a life-time. It can only be appreciated by touching it.

We were fortunate in having a letter of introduction to an artist, a Cuban gentlemen, who had resided in the city for many years. By his kindness and thorough knowledge of all that was worth seeing, we accomplished in our brief visit more than we otherwise could have done in a much longer stay. If one spot is to be selected as containing the master pieces of ancient sculpture and modern painting, it is the "Tribuna" in the Uffizi Gallery. In the center are five celebrated marbles; The Satyr, by Michael Angelo; a group of Wrestlers; The Medici Venus, found at Rome in 1680; The Grinder, whetting his knife to slay Marsayas, also found at Rome in the 16th century; and an Apollino, or young Apollo. Paintings by the hands of Raphael, Titian, Paul Veronese, Durer, Perigino, Michael Angelo and others, are hung about the walls; names that have become as familiar as household words in the world of art and beauty. In all the galleries, artists, or students are at work, copying the great productions of the masters. Some are so beautifully done none but a connoisseur could discern between them and the original. These copies may be bought at very reasonable prices. All students of art are allowed to paint in the galleries, after complying with certain prerequisites.

Of the city of which I should say much, I can say but little. I have not the pen of a poet, nor the descriptive power of an artist. "Beggar that

I am, I am even poor in words," to tell of all we saw and enjoyed in this delightful spot. Memories of others may fade, but Florence is locked within the strong towers of my heart.

Florence ranks with Rome, Naples and Venice in its many attractions. Lying on both banks of the Arno, it is "beautiful of situation and altogether lovely." We left it with regret, I with more than regret, for here I parted with the "pretty sister," and have not received a letter, or a photograph from her since. My wife has, but in it the "sister" makes no particular or special mention of me, other than to say, to be remembered. Thus another of my idols is shattered. I'll look about, however, for a new one. I shall call her Florence henceforth, for to my memory she brings back so many pleasures and so much of art. I have insinuated to Mary it would be the proper thing to invite her to visit us, but she doesn't enthuse much. I wonder why it is?

CHAPTER X.

VENICE.

"She that was fair, and never proud."

WE made many stops at various places en route between the Capitals, a history of which is of no special interest to the reader of this book. They were merely rests in our journey. They contained much to excite our admiration and added to our enjoyment. At Bologna, we ran into an Embassy from Chili, South America. The Valet to his Royal Nibs the Ambassador, had become all mixed up with the guards of the train. The trainmen could not speak Spanish, and the Valet could not understand Italian. I straightened out matters to the satisfaction of all, by my knowledge of Castillian. Speaking of languages, I was longing for the time when we should reach Germany, as I thought there I should be at home as far as the lingo was concerned. I made a slight mistake, or over-rated my abilities. I can speak German, that is to a reasonable extent, or as long as a native confines himself to an unabridged dictionary, but when he hurls a university at me I fail at times to comprehend his entire meaning. German in Germany, is somewhat different from the dialect spoken in the beer saloons of my town. It runs together more and gets over the ground faster. I always made them think I understood them, and when Mary asked for a translation, I told her what seemed best fitted to the circumstances. It did no harm and she was satisfied. She is a great admirer of linguistic attainments and wishes to take lessons of me. My rates, however, are too high. I have advised her to go to a kindergarten, or she might visit the Professor. The "sister" may visit me in her absence.

Venice has no trotting circuit. It is said there is but a single horse in the livery, and that is only shown on state occasions. It is a poor place for bicycles, you are obliged to dismount so often. Venice is a spot in which to love and linger. I could have hugged a door post, if Mary would not have been jealous. We arrived at 2:10 P. M., having left Florence at 6:10 in the morning. We were met at the station by a Gondola, (pronounced, *Gun*dola, the accent on the Gun,) and taken to the Grand Hotel by way of the Grand Canal. I might say every thing was grand while we were here. The sensations were novel, especially to Mary. The gondola was a dwarfed approach to the ship, only there was no smoke-room. We were asked not to forget the poor gondolier; we did not, we gave him some of the chicken feed. Whenever the gondola starts from a pier, or lands at a doorstep, a lot of beggars are around holding long poles with a hook on the end to steady the boat when you get in, or disembark. It is their profession, and from the exercise of it they get money, (enormous sums I presume,) and in the course of time have enough to build a Palazzio. Land must be cheap, as there is none. It is a queer place, full of history, Byron and Browning. I saw no Moors, no Desdemonas. Merchants more than sufficient. They are the same rascals, almost as bad as those at Gibraltar, and that is saying a great deal. They never let you out after entering their shops, and you can make the price before leaving, they'll take it. I have perfect confidence they would take anything—even a man's character. One day I saw a pipe in a shop window that caught my fancy, I went in to enquire the price, which the salesman told me was seven dollars. I offered him eighty cents and got the pipe. This is what they consider good business.

The city is built chiefly on piles, being six and a half miles in circumference, standing on 117 small islands formed by 150 canals, and connected by 378 bridges. How's that? Among the houses and at what seems to be the rear, extends a labyrinth of lanes paved with stone, brick, or asphalt, and alive with picturesque and busy throngs. It is possible to walk over the entire city by means of these passages, some of which are too narrow to be called even lanes. They are simply cracks between the buildings.

Our first ambition was to take a sail, or row, or whatever you choose to call it. You stand on the steps of your residence and call out "Poppi." A boat starts toward you at once. They are like all you see in the picture books, some more ornate than others, some open, some with little cabins or canopies. The engines are different from those you see in the Opera. They wear no gold belts, or plumes, or velvet coats. Most are in their shirt-sleeves, and the rest of their attire is third-hand. They stand at the stern holding a long oar, which is locked into the stump of an old tree, (that is what it looks like.) If you want to waste money, you may have two of these propellers, one however, unless there is much wind, being sufficient. These oarsmen are very expert, turning corners and passing other craft so closely, it would seem as if a sheet of writing paper could not be placed between, yet they never foul, or meet with any accident. The speed is ancient. So much so, that steam propellers have been placed on the streets (?) to enable men of business to reach their offices sooner. This permits them to lie in bed longer in the morning, a very wise and healthful habit. It spoils the poetry of the scene, however. Every day, almost every hour we sailed, for it was the only way in which we could get about in comfort. Sometimes we walked through the lanes, just to keep our legs in practice, but the going over so many bridges was tiresome. You go up half a dozen stops, then over the platform, then down. In about every forty feet you do the act again. This goes on as long as you walk.

The center of attraction is the Plazza of St. Mark. Here are the steps arranged along each side, where all sorts of merchandise are sold (generally yourself in the bargain) at the most extravagant prices. Here you feed the pigeons which swarm in thousands about you, alighting on your head and shoulders, showing no fear. None is allowed to be killed. They soil everything, and were a nuisance, though a pretty sight. Romantic young people, newly wedded couples in particular, are frequently photographed with the doves clustering about them. It looks pretty, but does not disclose their sweet relationships at home.

The church of St. Mark, the tutelary saint of Venice, and whose bones are said to have been brought here from Alexandria in 829, is the great building. It is decorated with lavish and almost Oriental magnificence. It is in the shape of a Greek cross, covered with Byzantine domes in the center and at the end of each arm, smaller ones at other points. Externally and internally it is adorned with 500 marble columns, mostly Oriental, with capitals in an exuberant variety of styles. The interior is profusely decorated with gilding, bronze and Oriental marble. In front are the four Horses, which probably once stood upon the triumphal arch of Nero, and afterwards on that of Trajan at Rome. They have traveled quite a little, Constantine having sent them to Constantinople, whence the Doge Dandolo brought them to Venice. Napoleon took them to Paris, but they were returned by Emperor Francis. The mosaics, both on the exterior and in the interior, are magnificent.

Opposite St. Marco is the Campanille. The Clock Tower is on the opposite side. The Library building consists of a double colonnade of arches and embedded columns. Farther on, are the two granite pillars erected in 1180. One bears the Winged Lion of St. Mark, the other St. Theodore on a crocodile. Between these two columns, executions took place in the olden time.

The palace of the Doges, founded in 800, is a remarkable building. It is decorated with foliage, figures of men and animals. A richly ornamented flight of stairs, called the Giants Staircase,(Scala dei Giante) derives its name from the colossal statues of Mars and Neptune at the top. These stairs lead to the entrance of the Palace. The interior of the palace is filled with paintings by Paul Veronese, Titian, Tintoretto and others equally celebrated. On the end of one of the galleries, is frescoed the largest painting in the world. It is called Tintoretto's Paradise. The number of figures is bewildering, many of the heads said to be admirable portraits. Another picture of interest is a "Last Judgment" by Palma Giovane with portraits of his wife in Heaven, Purgatory and Hell. She may have deserved all three. The Bridge of Sighs which connects the Palace of the Doges with the Prison, is always regarded with much sentiment. It is a waste of good material. Howells says, "It has probably never been crossed by any prisoner whose name is worth remembering, or whose fate deserves our sympathy." He never met me, I'm married. The Academy is another fine structure. It contains much of interest in the way of furniture, paintings and sculptures. The Grand Canal is lined with palaces and celebrated buildings, centuries old, and innumerable churches dedicated to various Saints all adorned with statuary, paintings, mosaics and works of art beyond compare. The house occupied by Byron in 1818, the home of Browning, and others of greater or less note. The Rialto crosses it midway between the Custom House and the railway station. It is flanked by shops, and looks as it always appears in the photographs. Shakespeare speaks of the Rialto in the Merchant of Venice, but it was not the bridge to which he referred, but the district, as the Rialto was the site of the ancient city of Venice.

Our evenings we would spend on the Plazza of St. Mark, listening to the music, sitting at little tables under the clear, full moon, which shone at its brightest for us, drinking light wines, or eating ices, or we would sail along the canals, out to the Adriatic, too enraptured by the beauty around us to talk. Everywhere, after the sun had gone down, there was music. Gondola after gondola passed to and fro, decked with colored lanterns, the occupants singing, or playing on instruments, the flute, the violin, or the guitar, all making merry under the glorious light, a sort of Fairy land, a living Opera, an ever-changing panorama, beautiful beyond description. There came over us a feeling, as if we could never break the silken bands that held us here.

One afternoon we spent at LIDO, half an hour away by gondola. It is the watering place of Venice, and from it may be obtained an excellent view of the old town. The beach is fine, and many were enjoying bathing in the surf. I saw a number of Venetian belles indulging, and wanted to go in so I might save their lives if they went beyond their depth. Mary would not allow me. She doesn't appear to realize my mission is to save life. Like every other spot in Italy, Lido has churches galore, belonging to the Saints, filled with pictures and relics. We did not buy any.

While we were here an American Man of War came into the harbor. I must say I felt my oats. We met the commanding officer while we were out for a walk, that is, in the way they walk in Venice, sailing along in the ship's gig, manned by hardy American Tars. Never to me did the flag appear so beautiful, flying full length at the stern.

I doffed my hat, Mary waved her handkerchief, and the Officer who was accompanied by what evidently was the American representative at this post, returned the salute. I felt safer that night, and proud. I could have thrashed the whole blasted nation, Mary into the bargain, though she is larger than I. At the Grand Hotel where we had our rooms, we ate in what was said to have been one of the apartments of Desdemona. Whether her bed-room, or parlor I know not. It was very gaudy and as lonesome as any such place in a foreign hotel. I often wished Des was there. I could have got along without Mary, for one meal at least.

As I was walking through the Grand Hallway of the hotel one evening, I was suddenly brought to a standstill by a slap on the back. I thought it was Mary. Immediately after came the salutation "Hello, Doc!" I turned and found one of my fellow pill-peddlers, much younger than I, once a resident of my city. We revived old times and absent friends at the proper counter, and resolved to see each other later. We did, several times. It only goes to show how well I am known all over the world, or how small the earth is.

Of course Mary dragged me into all the lace factories, paid double for little handkerchiefs, with no spot on which to blow the nose, "showers," not "blowers," bought a lot of dress-goods I could have packed into my pockets, and which cost a small bank, and then gave them away on arrival home. This is the penalty we men pay for what is called "Love." It will be a dead loss to her if she keeps on, as life insurance premiums will be passed and policies will lapse. I only purchased a few photographs and some bier.

CHAPTER XI.

MILAN.

"His neck erect amid his circling spires."

FROM Venice we went to Milan. I wanted to stop at Padua to get some fiddle-strings, and at Verona to see the two gentlemen of whom Shakespeare speaks, but Mary was opposed, so as usual I let her have her way. The ride was full of interest, of ever-changing scenes, all new and of a character different from any we had thus far seen. We were at the border of the Alps, at its feet, and the contour of the country began to partake largely of mountainous formation. Thus far we had enjoyed none but the finest weather, not too hot, with a few days of rain, only mere showers, just enough to lay the dust and cool the atmosphere. The days seemed very long, not tedious, as twilight lingered late into the night, so that at ten o'clock it was bright enough to read without the use of candles. It is certainly not so at home, and I shall ask the Professor the reason when next we meet. Our hotel was in the Piazza del Duomo, the focus of commercial and public life. Here is the great Cathedral, the eighth wonder of the world, and the largest excepting that at Sevilla, in Spain, and St. Peter's at Rome. It is built entirely of marble, roof and all, and is adorned with upwards of 4500 statues and 98 turrets. The stained glass windows in the Choir are said to be the largest in existence. The dome is 220 feet above the pavement, and the tower 360 feet above the ground. We took a long walk in the evening, looking in at the shops and wishing our letter of credit were heavier. In the morning immediately after breakfast I went to the Cathedral, intending to go to the top. Mary did not care to undertake the lofty ascent of 194 steps inside, and 300 outside the edifice in order to reach the summit. There was no "lift." I secured a guide and went up. The view beggars description. To the left (S. W.) was Monte Viso, then Mount Cenis, lower down the Superga near Turin; Mount Blanc, Great St. Bernard and Monte Rosa; then the Materhorn, then Cima de Jazzi, Stalhorn and Mischabel. To the Northwest, Mount Leone, and the Bernese Alps. At the North, the summits of St. Gotthard and Splügen. In the East, the Ortler. South, the Certosa of Pavia, in the back ground the Apennines. It was a beautiful clear morning, and the sky without a cloud. On the roof I met a family holding what we call a pic-nic. The guide told me they were there for the day, and that it was a frequent resort (the roof) for such outings. The only real loss

I sustained during my entire journey occurred here. I lost one of my gold sleeve buttons somewhere in or on the church. Its disappearance was not discovered until my return to the hotel. I did not go back to look for it. Steps and Italian robbers being too much in favor of my not seeing it again.

The interior of the Cathedral is supported by 52 pillars, each 12 feet in diameter, adorned with canopied niches with statues instead of capitals. The pavement is of mosaic, in marble of different colors. In the treasury is the mumified body of St. Borromeo, dressed in his Bishop's robes. It cost me a dollar, American money, to see him. Milan has eighty churches, enough to make the populace better than they are. Many of these houses of worship are very celebrated. All are filled with the usual pictures of Saints, Madonnas, Crucifixions, Resurrections, and what nots. Nearly all are of the Catholic persuasion. Here, as elsewhere, the arrangement for the stockholders differs from our own, especially in the larger ones. There are no pews, or cushioned seats, or foot-stools, or any such conveniences for a nap during the service. Benches or chairs which may be removed at will, are placed in the main aisle. Often there are none at all. You stand around, or kneel on the bare floor. All the collections appear to be wasted on ornamentation, or buying a picture, or statue of a new saint. I think it would be more christian to pay the minister, and get comfortable seats for the sinners. Everywhere about are little altars, or stations, dedicated to some particular Virgin, and at which service is held on certain hours, or days. You enter a church, walk about, see the entire museum, while the religious performance is going on at the same time at one of these little altars. As a rule no admission fee is charged. You give something in the shape of money to some one anyhow, even if it is only to the decrepit old woman, who holds back the heavy leather curtain at the entrance, as there are no doors. We went to lots of them and wasted our liras. Perhaps I may see some benefit to Mary after so much devotion. The period of incubation, however, is long.

One of the most interesting of the churches is S. Maria delle Grazie, founded in the 15th century and attributed to Bramante. It contains frescoes by Ferrari. In the old monestary, is the famous "Last Supper" by Leonardo da Vinci. This painting is fast showing the ravages of time, and is now nearly obliterated. It was painted in 1499. Many copies of the original are in the same room, made by celebrated artists, to facilitate the study of the work. There are in the city many charitable institutions, museums, palaces, theaters, gates and public works.

La Scala Theater, built in 1778, after a design of Piermarine, has the largest stage in the world, and on it some of the greatest lyric artists have made their debut. I went all over it, into the boxes, royal and plebian; into the seats, and recited what I knew of the Declaration of Independence on the stage.

The Galleria Vittorio Emanuel was directly opposite our hotel. It is in the shape of a Latin cross, covered with glass, and above the center a cupola. It is the largest in the world and beautifully decorated, filled with statuary, while all about are shops for the sale of everything, from a toothpick to a shoe lace. It opens into the plaza where La Scala is situated. Mary could not resist temptation, so bought a watch that she might know what time I recahed home when in Paris. I see no other reason for the purchase.

The streets of Milan are built to be used. Most of them have laid on either side near the sidewalk two flag stones, two feet in breadth, and between them small cobbles. This enables the vehicle to run on a smooth surface, while the horse has a firm foot-hold on the pathway in the center. Most of the wagons are for single horses. I wrote home to our Commissioners of Public Works, as new pavement for our streets was to be put down, giving them this idea (no charge), but they did not take to it. They, like many others, have much to learn. Next door to our Hostlery was a glove shop, with a pretty girl in attendance. I told Mary I needed gloves. She said I had a sufficient number of pairs in the bag. She, however, went in and let the darling squeeze her hand and fit a pair. All I got out of it was the bill. I am going to Europe alone next time.

As the King was to unveil a statue of Victor Emanuel in the Piazza del Duomo, immediately in front of the Cathedral and almost at our very door, we decided to get away a day earlier than anticipated, fearing the crowd and general rumpus attendant on such an event. Then, too, Mary might get lost.

The square had been fitted up for the Royal Family with booths, seats, flags and other decorations, suited to the occasion. We saw the monument as it was being covered with the white sailcloth, which was to be removed by the hand of the ruling Monarch at the proper time. I thought there were already a sufficient number of these "Forget-me-nots" in the city, but they have a mania, all over Europe, as soon as a man of any distinction dies to honor his memory with a big obelisk in some form. They have greatness thrust upon the m after death, if they did not deserve it in life. I wonder if they know it, and appreciate the devotion and how much it costs in money, time and fuss? I'd like mine put up while I am alive. It would be more satisfactory. Dr. Oliver Wendell Holmes says :

> "Isn't it a pity, a fellow can't hear what is said
> About a fellow, when a fellow's dead ?"

From some of the obituary notices I have read of men I knew in life, I have been sorry I was not aware how many virtues they possessed. They write up as angels. I sometimes have a different opinion, but never express it to the family of the deceased.

The Cemetery is one of the most beautiful in the world, almost as beautiful as the Campo Santo at Genoa. It is filled with Mausoleums, of the purest marble, and decorated by art in every conceivable shape and manner. Statuary is not so abundant as at Genoa, but the vaults are models of the sculpture's genius.

CHAPTER XII.

LUCERNE.

"Loveliest valley of the plain."

I NEVER was greatly entranced by Natural Scenery. Perhaps the fact has been due to the limited opportunities I have had of studying it. I prefer Archæology, Post-mortems, Coroners' Inquests and Railroad Accidents. Mary dotes on it. She spends half her time at home, looking out the back windows into the gardens of her neighbors, counting their chickens, and ash-piles, or watching the Health Board wagon gather up the refuse. Mary and I held a full hand, with both bowers, in our ride from Milan to Lucerne. I own up, much has been lost to me in not investigating the subject. I know a limited amount of geology, and work now and then on the lawn, when the coachman and gardener, my alter ego, is otherwise employed. I am careful not to do too much, especially with the mower, as over-rest in my alter ego's anatomical contrivance tends to apoplexy. I hire him by the month, and want to get full value.

We arrived at Lucerne in the evening, (7:30) just as the sun began to sink behind the great mountain tops, gilding the snow and ice upon the great heights, making them look as if crowned with gold. I shall never forget that afternoon. By means of an additional souvenir to the guard, we secured an observation car. It consisted of the same units as other cars, with the exception that on one side was a platform, three or four feet wide, with a railing around, so that by stepping from the compartment you were on the main deck and could look all about you. It gave a larger horizon, and rested your legs. I must refer you to some book of travel to describe the royal magnificence of the scenery that greeted us as we wended our way along the Alps to our destination. Great mountains on each side, here and there a Pass, now over a running river, made from the melted snows of far-off hills. The spot where the gallant little band of Swiss held their own with Spartan courage against the Austrians, little huts and hamlets, gardens rich in every kind of fruit and flower and herb, exhaling their sweetness on the air. Now down into a valley, then along the banks of a stream, then climbing to a higher plain, all painted by the hand of nature, more beautiful than the works of man, more glorious than any art. As we rode on we would catch sight of a little chapel, away up among the fleecy clouds. After a few moments it was at our side, and we could look within the doors ; then we bade it farewell, as we looked down upon it deep in the valley beneath, we mounting upward and onward. By the lakes of Como, Lugano and Marjiore we sped, diamonds in an emerald setting, sheets of water dotted here and there with villages at the feet of the great mountains, the mountains holding them and the sweet waters, as it were in the palms of their mighty hands. How beautiful they were!

We went through the great St. Gotthard tunnel, nine and a half miles long and twenty-eight feet wide and twenty-one feet high. It has a double track, is pitch dark, and becomes filled with smoke in the transit. There are lanterns on either side, but they serve no useful purpose. All the windows are ordered to be closed on entering and the guard generally does it for you. I was so interested in the scenery I forgot it. The guard smelt the mistake, and came in and did it for me, at the same time calling the windows bad names, and using language I presumed was intended for the benefit of the tunnel. That is what I supposed he was saying from the excited manner of his tongue.

We passed through many Swiss villages, stopping now and then for refreshments, or to add another locomotive as the ascent grew more and more abrupt. At Fluelen we took the boat and sailed the entire length of the lake of the Four Cantons, often called Lake Lucerne. Just before reaching Fluelen we stopped at Altdorf, which figures so conspicuously in the story of William Tell. Here Gessler ruled, and here the famous cross-bow man's arrow pierced the apple with a well-directed aim. A fountain now stands where the boy was bound. As we sailed onward to our destination, we passed or landed at many places of historic interest. Tell's Chapel was one of them. Here Tell escaped from the boat in which Gessler was carrying him to prison.

Then came Sisikon, then Brüneen. Beneath the Crags at our left is the Rütli, the most sacred spot in Switzerland. Here on the 7th of November, 1307, was formed the league against the tyrannous rule of Austria. It is a national place of pilgrimage, and is much frequented by societies and schools. At this point a crowd of children came aboard with their teachers, evidently a Sunday School excursion. They sang the entire way to Lucerne. The tune they seemed most to enjoy was what we call "America." I did not know the words, or what they were singing about, but joined in and helped out the chorus. They clustered about me as soon as they heard me singing, and I told them how I had a Sunday School Class at home in far off America, and lots of other things they did not understand, to match the conundrums their teachers gave them, and which wise adults cannot solve. Treib came next, with its old wooden inn, near to which is a pyramidal rock 85 feet in height, known as the "Mythenstein." It bears an inscription in honor of Schiller. In rapid succession are seen Gersau, Beckenreid, Bouchs, Vitznau, Weggis and at last Lucerne.

The steamers are much like those on the Thames. The captain was a big fellow, with more abdomen than anything else. His uniform outshone that of an American Admiral, and his voice sounded like a clap of thunder, as he shouted some unintellible gibberish down the tubes to the engineer. They do not use bells to communicate with the engine room, but yell out what is wanted. I could have understood the language of bells much better. The steering wheel lies flat, that is with its edge to the sides of the boat, not the plane of its greater surface toward the rail as with us. Two, or three men work at it. I enquired why they had it so, and received for an answer "they always had it so." They expect to change soon. It was the same on the Rhine boats.

It is of no earthly use to try to impart by words even a part of the beauty through which we passed this day. I could not, if I knew how. Many have attempted to do it. I have read their glowing descriptions, but they sound as idle tales. How great, sometimes, is the poverty of language. We met in our car during the journey a most intelligent English lady who had been a resident in and about this part of Lombardy, and Switzerland for many years. Her explanations and knowledge added much to our enjoyment. I only wish I could see a way to thank her in this book. We did not offer her money as she was "to the manor born."

LUCERNE is situated in the heart of Switzerland, and is the point to which all who travel converge. Once it was not as now. In the early days, when mountains, rivers and lakes were regarded with feelings of terror, a little assemblage of fishermen's huts stood on the banks of the Reuss. Its first important event was the founding of the convent of St. Leodegar about the year 735 whence the name of Lucerne is said to have been derived. When the peasantry in 1332 concluded the alliance out of which grew the Swiss Republic, its history was that of Lucerne. At the time of the Reformation, it remained true to the faith of its fathers, and still maintains its reputation as one of the strongholds of the Catholic faith in Switzerland. Its situation is wonderfully picturesque. On one side stands Rigi, on the other Pilatus, and between them the gleaming expanse of the Lake of the Four Cantons, with the snow range of the Alps beyond.

Our hotel, "The Beau-Rivage," was admirably situated on the border of the lake, Rigi, before us, Pilatus at our right. In front was the Quai National and a summer garden, where each afternoon an orchestra played, the music of which could be plainly heard in our apartments. It was a most excellent hotel, and I advise any who visit Lucerne to take their body and traps there. Here, as elsewhere among the Alps, is much to cause wonderment and surprise. It would be impossible for me to enumerate every place and spot of interest. There is the Post and Telegraph building, a fine edifice. The Hofkirche of St. Leodegar, is the principal church in the city. You enter it by a long flight of stone steps. It is full of history. The Choir stalls are beautifully carved, the wrought iron screens and baptistery being works of consummate art. On the side altar, are wood carvings dating back to the 15th century. Then a magnificent organ, which I had the pleasure of hearing, more by accident han by design. I am told it has 90 registers, and the Vox-humana and Vox-angelica enchant every lover of music. Concerts are given here every evening of the week. Behind the church is the ancient grave yard, surrounded by an arcade. To the North, in a romantic nook is the "Lion of Lucerne," sculptured by Ahorn, in 1821, after a model of Thorwaldsen, cut in the solid rock. In speaking to my son-in-law regaring it, he asked "out of what else could they have cut it?" He is in the rubber manufacturing business. Desiring to compliment him I suggested, had he been on earth, they might have made it out of some of his stock. He replied, he made "rubber to sell, not to last." They were wise to have it made early. Had he been in the world he might have taken the contract for the job, and where would it have been now? About the monument we read the simple legend, *"Helvitiorum fidei ac virtute,"* together with the names of fallen officers. It is commemorative of the struggle with the French, Aug. 10th and Sept. 2nd and 3rd, 1792. Close to the monument stands the Chapelle Expiatoire bearing the inscription *"Invictus Pax."* In the Museum, I saw many relics of the Lake Dwellers, their cloth, food, implements of art, war and industry, all laden with thought to those who are interested in the evolution of man. Beyond is the Glacier Garden, discovered by accident in 1872. Here are the "pot-holes" made by the waters of the glacier ages ago. Over the river Reuss is the old roofed wooden bridge the "Kapellbrücke," dating from 1333. It reminds one of the time when the town did not possess a single house of stone. That was, when Lucerne was known under the sobriquet of "the wooden stork's nest." In the one hundred and twenty-one triangular paintings, placed at regular intervals beneath the roof, the old Lucerners have celebrated the heroic deeds of the old Switzers, and the sufferings of their patron saints.

The Water Tower stands near. It is the remains of what was a part of the fortifications in the first half of the 13th century.

The Spreuerbrücke, or Muhlenbrücke resembles the Kapellbrücke in being built entirely of wood, and roofed with the same material. It is not so old by a century. It contains an interesting series of paintings by Casper Meglinger, dating from the 16th century, representing the "Dance of Death." There is a fine fountain nearby, called the "Fountain of the Weinmarkt." On the summit is a statue of St. Maurice, armed cap-a-pie, one of the finest ancient monumental fountains in Switzerland. Then the old Rathaus, the Musegg, the new Christ Church, built by the old Catholics of Lucerne, but in which the American Episcopal Church services are held.

The evenings here are like those in Naples and Venice, soft and pleasant. The leaves of the chestnut trees rustle in the breeze that sweeps gently over the rippling waters of the lake, and the peaks of the lofty snow-capped mountains flash and redden as though they were no longer cold, but glowing with an internal fire. The uplands seem all ablaze, while the shadows of evening are falling on the valleys. Softly swelling and dying gently away, the sweet tones of the vesper-bells are heard through the stillness of the night. Among the foliage of the trees, the electric lights flash, and on the lake the gondolas with their colored lanterns glide hither and thither, and the songs of their happy occupants are heard across the now dusky waters. "The Naples of

Switzerland" is a title Lucerne well deserves. Could I compress into a single sentence all the exclamations and all the thoughts uttered in the divers languages, it should certainly be this: How lovely is the earth, and how glorious is life.

One evening I had retired earlier than usual, tired by my walks and drives during the day, when Mary awoke me by calling out, "quick, quick!" I jumped out of bed, not knowing what had happened, or was about to take place. She simply said, "look, it is the largest comet I have ever seen." I looked. It was nothing more than a search-light on the top of Mount Rigi. I told her so, at the same time giving her my idea of her attainments in astronomy. She let me sleep after that.

We had intended to make some of the ascents, as it could be done easily by means of the cable cars. The day set apart for it proved hazy, threatening rain, so instead we paid our bill and turned our faces toward Munich.

CHAPTER XIII.

MUNICH.

"Here's to good old beer, drink her down."

ON this ride we made our only mistake of travel. We bought tickets for Munich, with privilege to stop over at Zürich. This I wished to do, as here it had been my intention to attend school, had not the Rebellion and the consequent premium on gold, put an end to such possibilities. It rained hard, so we gave it up, keeping on until we reached Romanshorn. When you buy a ticket in Europe, you are supposed to know when, and where to get out, and when, and where to change cars. We supposed we did. When we reached Romanshorn, we noticed most of the passengers left the car in which we were. We sat still, like "innocents abroad." Soon the guard came in to pick up in the way of valuables whatever might have been left by the forgetful passengers. I thought it a good time to begin the practical application of my knowledge of German. It was well I did. I asked if this was the train to Munich, and if we should remain seated. My want of a complete knowledge of the language prevents my repeating the entire conversation, but I understood he regarded us as escaped lunatics, and that if we did not "get up and git," we would spend the day in a spot not down in our itinerary. We got, (recht schnell) out into the pouring rain and into the proper Zug, and were hardly seated when the train moved on. A ride of an hour and a half brought us to Constance, on the border of a lake of the same name, over which we sailed to Lindau, where we again took the cars, reaching Munich at 7:28 P. M. As we were alighting from our carriage at the hotel, I was surprised and must say gratified, by the proprietor meeting us at the door of the coach. He grasped my hand and said in the best of English, "Dr. Piller, I am glad to see you." This was unexpected. I did not know my reputation had gone on ahead of my body. When I spoke to Mary about this remarkable notoriety, she said, "that's easily understood, he saw your name on the trunk." Thus one by one she breaks my idols. She is a regular iconoclast. I never think myself way up in "G," but she pulls the foundations from under, and I fall to her level.

When I got aboard of the boat at Constance, I roamed about to take in the machinery, look over the officers and see if a smoke-room was aboard, in order to insure a feeling of safety. During one of these pilgrimages, I thought to take a smoke. Accordingly I pulled out a cigarette and proceeded to hunt for a match. I found one and only one in my safe. I struck it, but a gust of wind quickly extinguished it. I used some polyglot in the English tongue, when a young gentleman standing near seeing my misfortune offered me another. I found he was an American, that is, one from Canada. Any one of the breed is acceptable at such a time and place. We at once struck up an acquaintance, and together traveled to Munich. He was a bright and most gentlemanly fellow, and we enjoyed his company. At one of the stations en route, we saw upon the platform a young lady waving an American flag, evidently to attract the attention of some expected friend. I wanted to be her friend, she was so pretty, and consequently took off my hat, waved my hand, and when Mary was not looking threw her a kiss. Our new acquaintance joined in the salutations for, he said, he was an "American in feeling and had great respect for the flag."

We were now traveling second-class (except on steamers, when we went first,) and found the compartments and service as good as first in Italy. During this ride, from Lucerne to Constance, we had as fellow-passengers a young woman and her little daughter, a child of some five years of age. I struck up a speaking acquaintance by petting the baby. It is a good way I find to reach a mother's heart. She gave me an Edelweiss, an Alpine rose, and traded a mark for one of our American silver quarters. Her husband, she said, was a petty officer in the army, and her brother a collector of coins. So am I, but not an officer, only a private in Mary's company. I am however, a numismatist, and accept with thanks any offering to my collection.

As I had rested all day in the train I went out in the evening with my new friend. Mary was tired. In fact it was better for her to keep quiet, and as a physician I advised her to do so. We had a good time viewing the city by gas-light as we could not during the day. We ran into some very good things, ending in the Concert Hall of the Löwenbräu-Keller, where a good band delighted our ears, pretty girls served the bier and sold ornamented postal cards which would have made Anthony Comstock blush. I had heard much of Munich bier and longed to sample it. I did, and long. We returned to the hotel before morning. Munich is the capitol of Bavaria, and has a lunatic for a king. It is built of bier, in fact, everything from houses to clothing has some of the article in their composition. They eat, drink, talk, smoke, do everything in bier. Breweries are everywhere. It was founded by Henry the Lion. It is difficult to tell what we did not visit. Among the many we did see (always having a guide,) were the monument of King Max Joseph, the Alte Residenz, built in 1596, with its four courts, one of which contains "Duke Christopher's Stone," the others filled with jewels, paintings and articles of virtu; the Festsaalbau; the Königsbau, built in imitation of the Pitti Palace at Florence, and where in apartments on the ground floor are the magnificent Nibelungen Frescoes by Schnorr begun in 1861. the Allerheiligen Hofkirche, or All Saints' church with its windows so concealed, as to cause the light to enter in a very effective manner; the Hof-und National Theatre; the Royal coach houses, and harness rooms. Among the most interesting objects in these latter are the state coaches and sleighs of Elector Max Emmanual, (1679); the carriage of Elector Charles Albert (1726), and the state carriages and sledges of King Lewis 2nd. The Hofgarten, the Musem of Plaster Casts, and the Ethnographical Museum.

The handsomest street is Ludwig-Strasse, originated by King Lewis 1st. Here are the Feldherrnhalle, the Church of the Theatines, erected in 1662, the Palace of Duke Max, the War Office and Kaulbad Museum, the Royal Library, Ludwigskirche, the Blind Asylum, the University, and last, as a fitting termination, the Siegesthor, or Gate of Victory. The Academy of Art is at the left. Maximilian Strasse is another beautiful way. Here is the Mint, the Government Buildings, the Bavarian National Museum, the statues of General Deroy, Schiling, and Fraunhofer, the optician. There is an elegant monument to King Maximilian 2nd, and a building

(Maximilianeum) founded by him for the instruction of students, who have shown an unusual aptitude for the civil service. There is also a statue of Elector Maximilian 1st, and palaces without number. Among them that of Count Arco-Zinneberg, and the Red Wittelsbach. In the Carolinen-Platz rises an Obelisk, 105 feet in height, cast from metal of captured guns, erected by Lewis 1st to the memory of 30,000 Bavarians who perished in the Russian War.

In one of the palaces, I have forgotten which, is a Throne Room. The Throne is guarded by a circle of ropes that it may not be defiled by the common people. That was not I. So I dodged under the protecting fence and sat on the Throne of Bavaria. I held the job only a short time, but it served to show an American could fill it. I could have run the whole country with a little help from Mary, and there would have been "a hot time in the old town that night." As I say, I did not keep my place very long. I wanted to run for office at home in the fall. One thing interested Mary. It was a bed-quilt which had taken forty women ten years to embroider. I thought it had been a waste of time, that might better have been spent in bringing up a family.

Of the collections of paintings, the Lotzbeck may be mentioned, but the finer is in the Old Pinakothek, which contains upwards of 1400 pictures, arranged in periods and schools. Every known painter and sculptor of world renown seems to be represented here. It is magnificent. The New Pinakothek, contains a wonderful collection of porcelains and paintings, though this latter is insignificant as compared to that in the old. The Glyptothek, is devoted almost entirely to ancient sculpture. The handsome Königsplatz, is terminated by the Propylæa, a magnificent gateway with Doric columns outside, and Ionic within. The Schack gallery is comparatively of no great moment. It was bequeathed by Count Adolf von Schack to the city. There are many other churches, museums and places of interest, too numerous for me to mention. Two I must speak of, Bavaria, and the Hall of Fame. It stands outside of the city about a mile and a half from the business center. It is a statue of Bavaria in bronze, 62 feet to the top of the wreath which the figure holds aloft. You may mount to the top, as I did. It resembles somewhat our statue of Liberty in the Harbor of New York. The other-master-piece, is the Hoffbräuhaus-Krug, or Royal Brewery. Jos. Wittman, Wirtschaftsführer, is the title of the owner, or bar-tender, I don't know which. It is on my bier-card, at any rate. Here I drank the best liquid bread I ever tasted, cooled down in the deep cellars, and frothing by natural methods, not by injected carbonic acid gas, and as pure as baking powder. It is entirely under government control, as are all the others. The bier is of a deep brown color, and only two cents a litre, (over a quart) too cheap not to have in the house, or to allow any one to starve. The brewery and saloon looked centuries old, black and dingy. It is built of stone, and in the center is a court paved with cobble stones. Here and there are barrels set on end to serve as tables, while around the sides are rough boards and seats to act the same role. Within are benches. Near to the center where the staff of life is sold, is an immense tank with a supply of running water. When you wish a loaf, you take down a Stein, wash it in the tank, so if it is not clean it is your fault, not theirs. Then walk without fear to the executive station, pay your Pfennigs and get your meal. After I had been there several times, I bought my mug and brought it home as evidence I had had enough to eat. It is one of my choicest treasures. I took the guide out one day to fill him up. I didn't do it, it almost worked the other way. We had a boss time, with no "don'ts." Mary was tired, so kindly remained at the hotel for a nap.

We did the town, including a show of Wax Works, in which an American lady took the part of snake-charmer. She had beautiful snakes, and was of fine figure. She out-stripped any snake-charmer I ever saw. I was glad Mary was at the hotel. Falling into conversation with her, she said she resided, when at home, on Second Avenue, near Fourteenth street. I told her I would call. She has not as yet informed me of her arrival, nor sent me her card. She is probably meeting with too much histrionic success to leave. I bought a lot of bier mugs as remembrances to my intemperate friends, and sent them home by express. I am sorry I did not wait until I landed in New York, as I could have purchased those manufactured in Ohio at a less price. They were too expensive for me to keep, so gave them to the above, as I said.

While here Grand Opera was being given in the Royal Opera House. We took it in, Tannhäuser. The Munichiners were trying to outdo the performances at Beyreuth, and I guess they did. It was great, especially the ballet. I took more interest in that than in the music, it was more anatomical. Mary insisted on having a box on so grand an occasion, and I lost so much in liquid bread. Women have no idea of economy, or of the real needful things in life. She drinks Chablis, and likes it. We had some washing done here. We had it done before, I mean of soiled clothing. They do it in great shape and cheaply. You make out your list, tell them when you want it, and the duds come up in immaculate whiteness. This is one advantage of living abroad. They have other improvements over our methods of doing things. After entering the carriage on our arrival, having first paid the entrance fee to the city, (no one gets in free, unless he has a pass, or is in with the gang) Mary asked if I had the umbrellas. I told her "no," and she commented on the fact, romanced on carelessness, forgetfulness, and advancing age, winding up by saying, "we shall never see them again." I might mention here, that it was her place to look after them, not mine, I had enough to do, looking after myself. I got out of the carriage and had a talk with the driver. He said, "come along, I guess we may find them." We went first to see if the train had pulled out of the yard. We found it had. He then took me into a little room, where on a rack I saw my lost goods, neatly wrapped up and labeled. I identified them, gave the fellow in charge a mark and returned to Mary to blast her with the result. It had not been five minutes since we left the train till I had them in hand. They had been gathered in by the guard, labeled with the number of the train, class, compartment, and a lot of other signs for identification. I'd like to see such a thing occur on an American railroad. The umbrellas are now safe at home. They are old and travel-worn, so we only use them on rainy days. One of the benefits Mary derived from her visit to Germany, was to find out that the word "lager" does not mean bier. She has found that it means a storage house. Now, since my return, I often go out to find a bread-lager, or a shoe-lager, or a lager alone. I tell you a tour in foreign lands is a great educator. It has been to Mary.

CHAPTER XIV.

VIENNA.

THE day we started for Vienna was remarkable for several reasons. It was a delightful Sunday morning, and the ride full of enjoyable views. Then it was my birthday, and last, I had a row with the Custom Officers. I may say in the beginning, I do not like the Austrians. Why, I cannot exactly tell, but they do not impress me as being truly religious. They boss a fellow too much, just as Mary does. I was anxious to see Vienna, and its renowned hospitals, for here Bilroth, one of the world's great surgeons, had held his clinic, and I had read much concerning his work. We found there was no change of cars, but a Custom House was to be passed. We took an observation car, and charged up the extra expense to coming patients. At Salzburg, on the border of the Austrian Empire, our baggage was inspected but, for what reason, I cannot tell. We had already been through so many Customs, and all seemed so farcical, this time I made up my mind not to bother personally about it. At Venice we were searched for sausages, they thinking we had our trunk stuffed with them from Bologna, and at Munich, for chickens brought from, I know not where, I gave the guard a florin and my keys, telling him to see me through. He took both. I remained seated in our compartment, supposing all was being done secundem artem. By accident, I happened to look out of the window and spied our trunk. They were going through it in a shape that excited my suspicions. I supposed the guard would see the Inspector, and the trunk would not be opened. It was his duty to do so, after getting that florin. I got out of the car, p. d. q., rushed into the Custom Room, and gave the guard my opinion of his executive ability. I got the affair settled by the payment of another florin, and entered the train as it began to move. I think there is such a think as being too conscientious.

Here everything German on the train changed and came under Austrian control. It was no improvement, at least I thought not after my experience. Salzburg had a lot to do in the time of the Reformation, burning heretics and such little matters. It wouldn't hurt it to do it over. They need reformation, and I am not so sure but a good roasting would be of benefit, anyway to the guards, and the Custom House officials.

We arrived at Linz soon after noon. Here I celebrated by birthday—not exactly in the manner I wished, but the best I could under the circumstances. I treated myself to bier, sausages, brown bread, and more bier. The latter made me feel like another fellow, so I took a drink with him. Mary decided not to join me, preferring to wait until we reached our destination, where, she said, she would "make me set it up for her." She did.

Vienna, or in German, Wien, is the capital of the Austrian Empire and is the grandest city, architecturally, I have ever seen. I doubt if there is a more beautiful one in this respect in the world. It is divided into the old and new Stadt. In the Ringstrasse are the Imperial residences, the houses of many of the nobility, the leading churches, museums, galleries, the Bourse, the Oriental museum, the University, the Rathhaus, with a tower, 320 feet high, the Court Theater, the splendid Houses of Parliament, the Palace of Justice, the twin Imperial Museums, the Imperial Opera House, the fittings of which are most sumptuous, without and within; the Commercial Academy, the Palace of Archduke William, the Austrian Museum, of Art and Industry, and the School for Art Industry. There are, moreover, medical colleges, hospitals, and extensive gardens. In architectural magnificence, it is not surpassed by any street in Europe.

Public Monuments are in the greatest profusion about the city. The most striking of which are, the equestrian statues of Joseph II. and that of Archduke Charles, Prince Eugene, and

Francis I. In the middle of the Graben is the Dreifaltigkeitssaüle (Trinity Column), erected by Emperor Leopold I. It was constructed in 1682 in memory of the Pest, and is often called the "Pestsaüle." The crowning work of all is the grand Maria Theresa monument. To describe it would take pages of this book. There are those to Beethoven, Haydn, Glück, Schiller and others, all of the greatest magnificence. Of the many fountains, the finest is that by Schwanthaler, representing Austria with the four rivers, Danube, Elbe, Vistula and Po.

Of the churches, St. Stephens is one of the noblest in Europe. The tower is 449 feet in height. The Capuchin church, contains the Imperial Sepulchre. Here the remains of the Imperial Family, from Emperor Mathias (1630) and his consort Anna (1619) down to our days, lie buried in one hundred and twelve coffins. We saw them all, and placed our hands upon those which contained the mouldering bones of Emperors and Kings. It now contains the bodies of eleven Emperors, fifteen Empresses, one King, two Queens, thirty Archdukes, fifty Archduchesses, two Dukes and two Princes. It also contains the hearts of Empress Claudia Filicitas, and Empress Amelia, the heart of Queen Maria Anna of Portugal, whose body is buried at the Theresian Nuns in Lisbon, and the intestines of Archduchess Henrietta.

They have queer customs as to burial of Royalty. As a rule the intestines of those buried in the sepulchre, are deposited in the Old Princes Crypt before the High Altar at St. Stephens, while their hearts repose at the Loretto Chapel of the Imperial Parochial Church of St. Augustine. Among the metal coffins here placed is many a precious work of art. One is the gigantic coffin of Empress Maria Theressa and her consort Emperor Francis. Pope Pius VI visited the sepulchre in 1783, and Napoleon descended into the graves of the Hapsburg dynasty. Touched by the sad spectacle of earthly transientness, he is said to have exclaimed, "Vanitas Vanitatum—hors la force." It is a solemn place. After life's fitful fever, here sleep those who have ruled empires by a nod, and shattered thrones by a word. They sleep, their burdens for a pillow, the same unbroken slumber which shall come to all. I could not but think of the emptiness of all earthly glory and honor, and made up my mind to have a good time here on earth, as I should be a long time dead.

Of the modern churches, the Lazaristenkirche, (the Votive church) erected in commemoration of the Emperor's escape from assassination, the Altlerchenfeld church, St. John's and the Byzantian Synagogue are worth a visit. The Hofburg or Imperial Palace, occupied from the 13th century contains the royal treasury. Tickets must be obtained the day before in order to visit it.

Here, always under guard, are the Regalia and Sacred Relics of the Holy Roman Empire (German Nation). Among them, are the Imperial Crown of pure gold, with polished uncut precious stones, the Imperial Orb of unpolished gold, the swords of Charlemagne, St. Maurice and the Imperial Sword of Ceremony, the Book of the Holy Gospels, upon which the Emperor takes the oath before coronation. This last is said to have been found on the knees of Charlemagne, when his tomb at Aix-la-Chapelle was opened by order of Emperor Otto. The leaves are of violet parchment, the writing in gold. In another case are the Coronation Mantle, the Alba, a Coronation Garment like a surplice, and other robes, embroidered in gold, and adorned with precious stones. Here is the lance of St. Maurice, with a nail of the Holy Cross set into its body, a piece of the Holy Cross, only surpassed in size by that preserved at Rome, a piece of the Holy Table Cloth, which decked the table at the Last Supper, a piece of the Holy Apron used by Christ when washing the feet of His disciples, a fragment from the Manger in which Christ was born, a bone of the arm of St. Anne, mother of the Virgin Mary, three links of the chain which bound the Apostles Peter, Paul and John, a fragment of the garment of St. John the Evangelist, a tooth (molar) of St John the Baptist, a Reliquary containing earth saturated with the blood of the Martyr

Stephen, and the famous necklace of Marie Antoinette, upon which Dumas founded his celebrated novel. Beside all these are sceptres, staves of office, orbs, wands, robes and banners, all magnificent. Then there are crosses, civil and military, and orders of the Golden Fleece, and others, each masses of diamonds, rubies, emeralds, and precious gems. There are Imperial crowns, knots and buttons of brilliants, ornaments, neck-laces, fans and bracelets of untold value. The great Florentine Diamond is here, one of the largest in the world, being exceeded in size by four others only, weighing $133\frac{1}{3}$ Vienna carats. There is a golden rose from the Pope, the Imperial Baptismal Vessels and Christening Robes, with a host of other treasures that one must see to form an idea of what royal grandeur is. For the truth of the holy relics I cannot vouch. The other traps look as if they were genuine. I give them to you as we saw them. What more can you ask? The finest piece of sculpture in Vienna, we saw in the Church of St. Augustines. It is the tomb of Archduchess Maria Christina, executed by Canova.

The Prater is the finest of all the parks. It was the site of the Great Exhibition in 1873. Near the entrance stands the monument of Tegellhoff, an Austrian naval officer of distinction. The Volksgarten is another beautiful park. In it is the Temple of Theseus, modeled after that at

Athens, containing Canova's marble group of Theseus and Minotaur. The Stadtpark, with its elegant Cursalon is another, being a favorite resting place on summer evenings. I hardly know how to cease recounting all the wonders and treasures we saw in this charming city. As I have said before of these wonderful capitals, one must see in order to learn all they contain. Words are failures to describe.

A curious little thing is, the "Stock-im-Eisen" in the corner of the Equitable Life Insurance building. It is the trunk of a tree, covered by the heads of so many nails driven into it that no particle of the wood can be seen. According to one tradition the Vienna Forest extended in olden times to this very spot, and this was a Holy Tree which used to be beset with nails on solemn occasions. Another saying is, that the iron ring which encircles the trunk, and bears the date of 1575, and the initials of "H. B.," and the lock supposed to be inextricable, were made by one Martin Mux, and the nails have been driven into the tree by young locksmiths when they started on their travels from Vienna.

During my stay, I visited many of the hospitals, saw some operations, and tried to bring home in my brain a few of the microbes of greatness and knowledge. Perhaps I have. My observations in all the hospitals of Europe, (Italy, Germany, Belgium, France and England) is, that ours in

America are much better fitted up. As to practice we are their equals, if not superiors. Material is greater with them, by reason of population. I saw in Vienna some cases of fracture put up in a way that would in America bring a suit for malpractice. Many of their methods are ancient, if not crude; still they do good work, and add much to the knowledge of the sciences. The advance of science here is largely in the care of the government. The scientist is helped by the Crown, and he has no fear his family will starve while he is delving into the unknown. In America, and I may say in England, nothing is done by national aid to help discovery on these lines. A few individuals have given generously of their wealth to aid the car of progress on its march. That is all that has been done. He who would work out some of the great problems of life, must do it by his own hand, and at his own risk. No help is given him until he discovers something out of which money may be made. Experimental science is hooted at and the investigator called a fool. Science for the sake of Science, for the betterment of mankind, must take care of itself. It is a pity what I say is true. When the English speaking nations shall awake to a full appreciation of the value of Biology, Sanitation, Medicine and Surgery, upon the welfare, life and happiness of the people, something will be done. I, however, fear the time is a long way off. Mary is doing something at it, by holding the office of President of a Female Suffrage Club. From her wild talk, I am sure it is on the track of something that is to advance everything. If it finds it, there will be a scientific revolution, and we shall have things as they should be, so she says. She tells me she has some ideas. For my part, I know she has. I think them erroneous however.

I expected to drink the best coffee in Holland, as her colonies are supposed to produce the finest brands. I was mistaken. Vienna knows how to make it, the best I have ever drunk. Mary has never tasted coffee, so her opinion on the subject is of no value. She sticks to tea and other herbs. Since coming to Europe she has acquired a habit for Rhine wines and Chianti. Next she'll take to bier, and I shall be the only temperance person in the family. She need not preach W. C. T. U. after all I've seen. I have been graduated.

Vienna rolls are no different from any others I have seen or eaten. Perhaps they originated here, hence the name. They are no improvement over the old-fashioned biscuit, and twice as difficult to masticate. The water is abundant and delicious, the finest we tasted in our travels.

CHAPTER XV.

DRESDEN.

IT was so cool the evening we arrived in Dresden, the capital of Saxony, we wore wraps, though it was July. We had taken the precaution to secure an observation car, so we might see something of the out-door life of Germany. Mary slept most of the way, now and then waking up to say "don't," as she cares little for out-door work, or in-door either. The motion of the cars soothes her. Germany is a fine country, abounding in beet fields, from which the sugar used over nearly all of Europe is obtained. This variety is not so sweet as that made from the cane, but the difference is hardly appreciable. It is cut into small blocks, an inch long. half an inch broad, and a quarter of an inch thick.

Dresden is tame architecturally, after Vienna. It has been aptly called the "German Florence," by reason of the magnificence collection of pictures in the Royal Gallery. After the usual drive in the morning, visiting fountains, monuments, parks, gardens and terraces, we made haste to see the pictures and interiors of churches, palaces and shops. Mary is always losing something.

Here she lost her eye-glass hook. Ten cents purchased one good enough for some one else to find. She still has it for a wonder and a remembrance. There are many old and interesting bridges, especially the Marienbrücke, and the Albertsbrücke. Several of the chief attractions are situated close to the old bridge. The Brühl Terrace is one. Originally laid out in 1738, as a garden, by Count Brühl, it is now a favorite promenade. It is approached from the Schloss-Platz, by a broad flight of stairs adorned with gilded groups of "Night, Morning, Noon and Evening," cut in sand-stone by Schilling. At one side are the Brühl Palace, and the Academy of Art. Then is seen the statue of Semper, and the Rielschel monument, also by Schilling. The Albertum, originally the Arsenal, is now a gallery of Sculptures and Casts. Beyond is the Maurice monument to the memory of the Elector of that name, who fell in battle 1553. Near by are the Law Courts, the Church of St. John, and the Schilling museum. The Roman Catholic Court Church is opposite the old bridge, and is adorned with seventy-eight statues of saints, on the parapets and at the entrance. The Tower is 280 feet high. Beneath the sacristy are the royal burial vaults.

The Royal Palace, founded 1534, is an extensive edifice, filled with beautiful frescoes. Before it rises the loftiest tower in Dresden, 331 feet high. In the palace is the Green Vault, containing one of the most valuable existing collections of curiosities, jewels, trinkets, and small works of art, dating from the late Renaissance and Rococo eras. The cabinet of coins, in which I was much interested, is particularly rich in choice specimens. In the Theatre-Platz, is the fine equestrian statue of King John. The Hof-Theater, one of the finest in Europe. is lavishly decorated with paintings, and statuary. Among the statues are those of Goethe, Schiller, and Moliere, figures of Sophocles, Euripides, Shakespeare and others. The museum forms a wing of the Zwinger, erected in 1711. It and the museum contain the most important of the Dresden collections. The Picture Gallery in the museum now ranks with the Louvre, Pitti, and Uffizi, as one of the finest in the world, and all the great masters of the Golden Period of statuary and art, are admirably represented. Here I saw what to me was the most beautiful painting in the world, The Sistine Madonna of Raphael. In the words of another, it is one "in which the most tender beauty is coupled with the charm of the mysterious vision, forcibly striking every susceptible beholder, and the longer he gazes, the more enthusiastic will be his delight." The picture is the only one in the room, the light coming in so as to illuminate that most beautiful face, and the entire painting in a glorious halo. You sit at the end of the room opposite the painting, about twenty feet away. No one speaks, every voice is hushed before this master-piece of art. I wish I were able to tell how it impressed me. I have seen thousands of others, gems from the hands of the greatest painters, never one like this. I went back to the room again, and again, so fascinated was I, and as I looked upon it for the last time I gave a sigh of relief, as the strain upon me relaxed. Ask any one who has seen it. They will tell you the same story. Besides the paintings are tapestries, engravings, and everything beautiful in art.

Opposite the Zwinger, is the Prinzen Palace erected in 1715, the residence of Prince Frederick Augustus. Here also is the Sophienkirche, or Protestant Court Church. Near by is St. George's Fountain. Behind the Imperial Post Office is the Industrial Museum, containing furniture, bronzes, and pottery. In the Neumarkt, rises the Frauenkirche, erected in 1726, with a lofty dome 310 feet in height. In the Platz in front, is the Luther monument, a bronze cast from his original statue for the monument at Worms. A cross in the pavement near by, marks the spot where Crell, the Calvanistic Chancellor was executed in 1601. On the same square is the museum Johaneum, now containing the Historical museum, and collections of Porcelain. There are many other statues, and fountains, and public buildings. The old Palace Chapel, of 1555, the house of Carl Maria von Weber, the composer, the statue of Frederick

II, a figure of Germania, in Carrara marble, to the memory of the war of 1870, on the pedestal of which are allegorical figures of Peace, National Defence, Science, and Enthusiasm. The Kreuzkirche, with its tower 312 feet in height, attracts attention; likewise the Goose Stealer Fountain, the English church, with wonderfully beautiful stained-glass windows.

In the Neustadt, is the equestrian statue of Augustus II, "The Strong," as he was called, over life-size, erected in 1736, also the Japanese Palace, built in 1715, and named after the Japanese porcelain formerly preserved here. It is now the Royal Library. The Gardens are many, of which the Grosse Garten, Botanical and Zoölogical are the most deserving of notice. The Cemeteries have obelisks and contain the remains of many noted in art, war and theology. Dresden at one time was celebrated for the manufacture of porcelain, or as we call it, china. To a certain extent it still maintains its old reputation. We thought of buying a dinner service, but found the pieces could be broken as easily as those costing a dollar a dozen, instead of one hundred a plate. This in part led us to give up the idea. Mary says she would like to live in Dresden, "it is so peaceful." I wish she would. I prefer Munich, or Paris. There is more going on in them.

CHAPTER XVI.

BERLIN, POTSDAM, AND SANS SOUCI.

"UNTER den Linden," Berlin, and Sans Souci, had been familiar words since childhood. As our letter of credit was not exhausted, we felt the inhabitants would rejoice to see us. We went in, and struck Fourth of July. We registered at the Grand Hotel de Rome, on "Unter den Linden," near to Friedrichstrasse. I have described in other chapters the places we visited more fully than I intended when I began writing, so henceforth shall try to keep within bounds, asking the reader to look up points that may interest him in better and more fully descriptive books than this.

We had been expecting letters from home at each resting place, and thought we should surely find them here. We were again disappointed. Subsequently we discovered they had been written, but either traveled too slowly for us, or else some other distinguished Americans received them. I have always been suspicious they contained bills from my creditors, and that my son worked in with the Postal Officials at New York, and blocked the game. He always does right by his father. I have had him under the "X" rays, and find his liver and heart are like his mother's, but his brain and feet are like his father's.

The morning after our arrival, Mary broke down the elevator so effectually it did not run for two days. It may have been accident, but Mary and broken "lifts" are too common to be coincidences. As it happened on the glorious Fourth, she has always claimed the accident (?) occurred to celebrate the day. She had Fourth of July in several places, if this was the case. The weather was cold and threatened rain. In fact it was more so, and more of it than anywhere else. No letters and rain made us home-sick, and we wished ourselves at home in our own Palazzio Damfino, many times.

When you leave a train on entering Berlin, you see a policeman posted at the point of egress. He hands you a metal ticket with the number of a cab, the traveler having stated which class he desires. You give the medal to a porter, who will summon the proper vehicle, and see that your traps are put in. Of course you give both a remembrance.

Berlin is magnificent with its palaces, churches, and memorial buildings. "Unter den Linden" is the handsomest and busiest part of the city, flanked by magnificent palaces, spacious hotels, and attractive shops. It is about a mile in length, from the Brandenburg Gate to the Royal Palace, and 196 feet wide. Through the center runs a double row of linden and chestnut trees, making an avenue between. At one end is the Palace Gate with its eight groups of statuary, at the other the stately portal of the Brandenburg Gate, surmounted by a colossal chariot of Victory. The street reminds one of the boulevards of Paris.

At the east end rises the statue of Frederick the Great in bronze, probably the grandest monument of its kind in Europe. Near the statue is the palace of the Emperor William I. Opposite the palace is the Academy building; then comes the University, the garden of which is adorned with statues of William and Alexander Von Humboldt. The Royal Library is behind the palace of William I. The motto beneath the cornice, *"nutrimentum spiritus,"* was selected by the Great Frederick. Here are the first impressions of Luther's translation of the Bible, Melanchton's report of the Diet of Worms, Gutenberg's Bible of 1450 on parchment, the first book printed with movable type, and many interesting manuscripts. On the other side of the street is the Opera House, with groups of statuary pertaining to the Drama. Statues stand before the doors in the square. The Kaiservase, a huge vase with allegorical figures, is between the Library and Opera House. It was presented to Emperor William I, on his 90th birthday, by the Empress Augusta. Behind is the church of St. Hedwig, an imitation of the Pantheon at Rome. Then there are the Royal Guard House, Singing Academy, and the Arsenal. This latter contains a military museum and the "Hall of Fame." I was greatly interested in the collection of weapons, especially the cannon, mediæval and modern, many having been captured in the Franco-Prussian war, and bearing marked evidence of having taken part in battle. Among the number was one of American manufacture, a mitrailleuse.

The Hall of Glory contains statuary, paintings and frescoes upon the walls, illustrative of the progress of the German Empire. In a line with the prolongation of the Linden is the Schloss-Brücke. It is adorned with eight groups in marble, over life-size, illustrating the life of a warrior. To the right beyond the bridge, is the equestrian statue of Frederick William III, 20 feet in height. The pedestal has allegorical figures at the front. A little way farther on is a huge granite basin, said to weigh 75 tons, hewn out of solid rock. It is 22 feet in diameter. The Royal Palace was erected in 1443, by Elector Frederick II. It has been much altered since its beginning, and is still unfinished. At the portal is the statue of the Horse Tamers, in bronze, presented by Emperor Nicolas of Russia. In the first court is a bronze group of St. George, and the Dragon. The building contains 700 apartments, also a large number of portraits of the

Royal Family, ball rooms, picture galleries and statuary. In going through one of the apartments, I think it is the grand ball-room, the visitor is obliged to put on slippers made of felt. You do not pick out your size, but take them as handed to you. They are all large enough. I got Mary's. In them you shuffle, (you cannot walk) over the polished floor. I think this is done for two reasons. First, that you may not scratch the floor, the surface of which is like a mirror, and second, that you may help by your mode of movement, to enhance its lustre. It is a great game, and helps out the lazy janitor. I enjoyed it, as it was a real Yankee idea. There are an Old and New Museum, both filled with objects of great interest, sculptures, paintings, antiquities, coins, casts, etc. Their importance consists in the representation of the most varied styles, and epochs, rather than in the possession of masterpieces by great artists. Near the New Museum, in the center of the square, surrounded by Doric colonnades, and embellished with statues, flower-beds and fountains, is the National Gallery. It is filled with statuary and paintings.

Friedrich Strasse, was nearly opposite our Hotel. It is one of the chief thoroughfares, filled with life and bustle. I found in it a good place for bier but did not tell Mary. I went there often to acquire more fluency in the German language, and fluidity of German food. It was always a good starting place when I wished to go anywhere. It is the longest street in town. A little way from this street is the Gendarmen-Markt. In the center, now called the Schiller-Platz, are the Schauspiel-Haus, (Theatre), the French church, the New Church, and several handsome private residences of the last century, forming the finest architectural group in Berlin. In front of the Theater, (Schauspiel-Haus) stands the monument to Schiller, in marble, 19 feet high. Wilhelm Strasse, is considered the most aristocratic quarter of the city. Here reside the Royal Ministers, Princes, the Chancellor, and other high toned people. In the Wilhelms-Platz, are flower-beds, with statues of six heroes of the three Silesian wars of Frederick the Great. Here also is the Palace of Prince Frederick Leopold, the Kaiser-Hof, the church of the Trinity, and the Imperial Treasury. In the Leipzerger Strasse is the Concert Haus, the Equitable and the New York Life Insurance buildings, the General Post-office, Post-office Museum and War-office, the Hall of the Imperial Diet, and near at hand other buildings pertaining to the management of the government. In the Belle-Alliance-Platz is the Column of Peace, 60 feet high, erected to commemorate the 25th anniversary of the Peace of 1815, the Royal Porcelain Factory, the Monument of Victory, and the Mausoleum, where Queen Louise, and her husband, Frederick William III, repose. In the city are many other noted churches, schools, museums, exchanges, markets, theaters, parks, and palaces, too numerous to mention. We could not see them all in our brief stay, but we got over a great deal of ground. I have spoken in detail more than I expected. I trust it has not proved wearisome.

Soldiers are everywhere in Berlin. In fact you see them at all times, and in all places throughout Germany, and a fine lot of fellows they are. They march with a peculiar (to me) step, called "the Goose Step." The foot comes down flat upon the ground, after the thigh has been thrown forward at right angles to the body, and the whole leg pushed forward. In my experience in war and married life, I have seen nothing like it. Around "Unter den Linden," and within the circle of trees is a path, in which I saw the Cavalry manœuvering. Whether the path is for this sole purpose, I do not know. It appears so at any rate. I went to see the soldiers at the gymnasium, exercising before the drill began, and afterwards saw them going through all sorts of military tactics which made me think the Emperor had a fine corps of men, and that some nations would better go slowly before challenging them to fight.

On Sunday, we went to the great Fair just outside of the city. It was not a National one, but limited to the industries of Berlin itself. The buildings were large and attractive, a "World's (Chicago) Fair" in miniature. The displays were lavish, comprising every art, and manufacture, on exhibition and for sale. There were also the usual outside temptations, streets of Cairo, amusement halls, all that goes to make up such a spectacle. A large crowd was there, though it rained in torrents and was cold. I took precautions against the entrance of microbes, Mary took cold. It was a just punishment for breaking the Sabbath, and the effects kept her in bed for two days. I urged her not to go, but she persisted, saying she had reasons for not remaining at the hotel. I have always thought she suspected I had an engagement with some young lady. This condition of Mary, the broken elevator, and no letters from home, made her visit at Berlin rather doleful. We celebrated the Glorious Day without fire-crackers, but drank to the healths of President Cleveland and the Kaiser. I saw one United States flag flying over a hotel on "Unter den Linden" where many Americans were staying. This is all the celebration we had.

Mary being better by Tuesday under my treatment (for which she never paid me), we went over to POTSDAM, taking a train to the town, then a carriage and a guide. Potsdam is located 16 miles from Berlin, and is called the "Versailles of Prussia." While driving about, we met the royal carriage, containing the only daughter of the Emperor, with her maids of honor. At another time we ran across the Emperor's brother-in-law. I have forgotten his name. We did not recognize them, as we were too busy looking at other curiosities, and I had to keep an eye on Mary, fearing a sudden return of her cold. The Emperor was at home, but by some mistake had not received our cards or invited us to call. I harbor no ill-will.

Passing through the Brandenburg Gate, erected in the form of a Roman triumphal arch, with an allegorical fountain group of five figures near it, we entered the Park of SANS SOUCI. At this entrance is the Friedenskirche, or Church of Peace, the favorite building of Frederick William IV. A broad flight of steps ascends to the Palace. On the last terrace, Frederick the Great's greyhounds are buried. The king expressed a wish to be buried at the foot of the statue of Flora, which stands at this point. ("Quand je serai la je serai sans souci").

The Palace of Sans Souci is of one story, erected in 1745, and was Frederick's almost constant residence till death. His rooms are preserved nearly unaltered, and the main interest of the palace consists in the numerous reminiscences it contains of its illustrious founder. Among the treasures shown are, the clock he was in the habit of winding, and which is said to have stopped at the exact moment of his death, 2:20 A. M., August 17th, 1786, the chair in which he died, his spinet, together with his portrait, the only likeness for which he ever sat, taken in his 56th year. The room in which Frederick William IV died (kept unaltered) with that occupied by Voltaire may be visited. Pictures and busts are on every hand. The picture gallery itself contained little of interest.

On the way to the Orangery, we passed the famous windmill, which the owner is said to have refused to sell to Frederick. It is now however royal property. The Orangery contains a large number of paintings, mostly copies, and some statues, as Ceres, Flora, and a copy of the Farnese Bull. There are two ancient sarcophagi, used as troughs, near the steps, as you go down into the garden. The gardens about the palace are kept in the most careful manner, and are filled with vines, flowers, and fountains. I walked through them, but as it promised to be fatiguing to Mary, she remained in the carriage, meeting me at the other end. I was not alone however. Two pretty girls wished to place themselves under my care and you can wager I took care of them. We were some time in going through. A mile at least from the Orangery, is the New Palace, now the summer residence of the present Emperor. We did not stop. Returning to the town, where many army officers reside, we visited all places of interest. I remember a large iron gate, at the top of a terrace, which the guide told me had been opened but once, which was when Napoleon passed through. I do not call to mind just where it was situated, but think it was one of the entrances to the park. In the Lustgarten are bronze busts of York, Blücher, and twelve other celebrated personages, not of much interest, at least to me.

The Royal Palace contains many remembrances of Frederick. His flute, music-stand, ink-stand, autograph notes, traveling cup, the apartments of Frederick William I, and a few pictures painted by that Monarch, "in tormentis," that is, during an attack of gout. Of course there is much else to please, and charm the eye. Near by is the lime tree, now protected by an iron covering, under which petitioners gathered so as to attract the attention of Frederick in order to present their grievances. Here is the marble Mausoleum of "Unser Fritz," guarded by a soldier at the door. You are requested not to speak, while within, as silence seems to make the spot more sacred.

The Church of St. Nicholas is near. The Rathhaus, built in 1754, the gable of which is adorned with a gilded figure of Atlas bearing the globe. The Obelisk in front, 75 feet in height, is embellished with medallions of the Great Elector, and the first three kings of Prussia. Adjoining is the Barberini Palace, erected by Frederick in imitation of that at Rome. The hall is used for scientific and other societies. A vault under the pulpit of the Garrison church, contains the remains of Frederick the Great, and of his father, Frederick William I, founder of the church. I stood by the coffin of the King and Elector, on the spot where Napoleon stood, and where he is said to have uttered these words: "If you had been living, I would not have been here." I plucked a leaf from the wreath which is daily placed upon the coffin, and have it among the memorabilia of my travels. As if in keeping with the great soldier, there are many flags about the entrance of the tomb, flags captured in the memorable days of 1813-1815. After all "the path of glory leads but to the grave." There were other places of interest we failed to visit for want of time, much to our regret, as for instance Babelsburg. We returned to Berlin late in the evening.

Before I close this chapter, I cannot help speaking once more of the palace of the old Emperor William, grandfather of the present sovereign. An old woman was in attendance who had been a body servant of the old monarch. She was very kind, showing us many treasures of the old warrior, we might not have seen otherwise. His chair, his pen, his books, his private apartments, nearly everything which added to the enjoyment of his last days here in Berlin.

CHAPTER XVII.

FRANKFORT-ON-THE-MAIN. HEIDELBERG. MAYENCE.

It was a long ride, of more than twelve hours to Frankfort. A mistake was made in not cutting it in half, and stopping over night at Leipsic. I'll do it another time. Mary had fine innings at "don't," slept a good deal, ate at every station, while I smoked and looked out of the car window over the country. I thought of buying a farm. Mary was really ill, her cold still quite severe. These foreign microbes are more tenacious than ours. I had brought with me a supply of medicine to use as occasion required, and gave Mary a sample of all I had. I was bound to fetch *her* or the microbes. She was much improved when we reached Mayence.

FRANKFORT-ON-THE-MAIN, is a delightful little city. Though our stay was brief, we took in all points worth seeing. The chief were the Stadt Art Gallery, the Ariadneum, containing Dannecker's master piece of "Ariadne," the Palm Garden, the Kaisersaal in the town hall, with its portraits of German Emperors, the house where Goethe was born, the Schawnthalers monument to the poet, the monument to Gutenberg and Schiler, the old Bridge with its diabolical legend, the statue to Charlemagne, and the Cathedral.

Over the main entrance of a house (Swan Hotel) opposite our hotel, was a tablet stating, "Here on the 10th of May 1871, the treaty of peace between Germany and France was signed by Bismark and Jules Fevre." There are many gardens and fountains scattered through the city, which Mary wished to visit but was too ill to gad much, so I took a day off, and ran down to Heidelberg. I could in this way see some new things, have a time with the boys, and miss some hundred thousand "don'ts."

I bought a "Rundreise," or excursion ticket, as it saved a few marks for bier. I did this on the advice of my son-in-law, who had lived in Germany several years. I often wished for him, as he always helps "Pop" to have a good time. I met in my compartment going thither a young minister and his pretty wife, Episcopalians and from America. Of course I was in it. Unmarried, pious and an Episcopalian. We talked and talked, that is the pretty wife and I. As for the Dominie, I allowed him to read the newspapers, as it kept his eyes from us. I got off at Darmstadt, long enough to see the War Monument, but nothing else. A friend had given me before leaving home a card of introduction to an intimate acquaintance in this burg, but through some misfortune I lost it, and not remembering the name or address, missed a good opportunity, for I wanted to see the Library, and Picture Gallery, and in the palace of Prince Charles the famous Madonna with the family of Burgomaster Meyer. You can't have your own way, always. Misfortunes come to the good, as well as to the bad. Mary, you will remember, was ill at this time. It began to rain just as I reached HEIDELBERG, and I had no umbrella. They say it always rains here, but I did not know the adage till I reached the town. I started to engage a carriage, but so much was demanded for its use, I thought it would be cheaper to purchase a new suit of clothes, so left it and proceeded to walk up the hill to the Castle, taking things in as I passed along. After I had gone some distance, I saw the same turnout coming my way and an offer by the driver at a more reasonable rate, closed a bargain, and I got in. Soon after a guide appeared offering his services, and we made a contract on that. Everybody happy. We crawled up the steep hill to the old ruin, the finest in Europe, (though I began to think I was) passing little summer houses, and hotels, making me wish I might spend weeks among and in them. At the entrance to the Castle is a gate, and near by a café, into which I took the guide and blew him off a couple of times, and then went into the grounds. I told the coachman to reserve the carriage until I returned. I went all over; through the gate built in a night; enjoyed the charming view, which tempts you to linger, then into the Castle, half palace and half fortress, up into the museum, and down into the chapel and cellar, where is the celebrated "Tun." I was sorry it was empty. The last time it was filled three hundred and sixty thousand bottles of wine were said to have been put in. I am inclined to think this is either not true, or the bottles were small. However, it can hold enough to keep a poor family all winter.

The guide asked me if I desired to visit the Molkencur, or Milk Cure a short distance, he said, above the Castle. Two hundred feet up hill! I wonder what he calls long! I declined, telling him I had been weaned. Returning, I took the carriage and rode all through the town, over the Old and New Bridges; saw the University, the Church, half Protestant and half Catholic, and by this I mean, the building is in one piece, one sect worshipping in one end, the other in the other; the dueling rooms of the students, where are cut the names of many who have become distinguished in the world. I bought at the Castle a Stein for my son-in-law, who is making a collection of ceramics, and a metal mug for an intimate friend who never drinks. When I returned to Frankfort, Mary asked we where I was going to pack them, and why I had not brought a whole brewery. I declined to discuss the subject. Her cold made things look large. I did not feel very well myself going back, for I missed the company of the clergyman's pretty wife, and perhaps had walked too far. Mary said I had "been too kind to the guide." I recovered.

We left for MAYENCE, or MAINZ, take your choice—the next afternoon. It was growing warmer. In the evening of the day before we left for Cologne, we rode about the town, viewing the barracks, monuments, and attractive places. Mary being better so I could leave her without causing myself anxiety, and also being lonesome, I spent the latter part of the evening in a grand garden near our hotel. It was brilliantly illuminated, filled with families, fathers, mothers and children, from the grown up son to the nursing babe. An orchestra discoursed delightful music, and every one was having an enjoyable time. All were drinking bier like christians. I want to say right here, and Mary will bear me out in this assertion if in nothing else—we never saw a drunken person in our entire travel until we reached London. There the number of drunken men and women would shock a saloon-keeper. The Italians and Germans drink wine and bier as we do coffee and tea, not gulping it down, but sipping it. This is first, because they have not the money to pay for it, and second, they drink for the social feature, not to become intoxicated. We met two or three wedding parties holding a celebration in several hotels where we were staying, and though at times we could hear them talking and singing, as if they felt exhilarated, yet we never saw one the worse for his indulgence. Raines Bills are unknown, nor does a man abuse his liberty. I am in favor of their methods, and shall vote with the Germans at the next election.

To get back. The city is situated at the junction of the Main and Rhine rivers. A Roman camp was located here B. C., 38, but the foundation of the town dates from B. C., 14, when Drusus built extensive fortifications and added the Castellium, whence Castle takes its name. In the Citadel is an interesting monument, the Eigelstein, 45 feet high, erected by soldiers in honor of Drusus. Outside of the city are extensive remains of a Roman aqueduct. I did not see them. The Cathedral is one of the grandest in Germany, none so rich in monuments. The Brazen Doors bear inscriptions engraved in 1135, in honor of Archbishop Adalbert I. In the Chapter house, may be seen the tablet to the memory of Fastrada, wife of Charlemagne, and Schwanthaler's monument to "Rauenlob, the pious minstrel of the Holy Virgin, and of female virtue." (There never has been another born.) Near it is the older tombstone of 1783, a copy of the one set up at the death of the poet in 1318. Near the Cathedral is a statue of Gutenburg. There is an Electoral Palace, St. Stephen's Church and others we did not have time to visit. I had a circus in the town trying to buy some cough-drops for Mary. I wanted troches, but the apothecary insisted on giving me stuff in a bottle. At last I succeeded in obtaining some malt drops, like candy, which seemed to allay the irritation in Mary's breathing apparatus. I could not work my M. D. as I had no license to practice in the country, so was obliged to pass my myself off as an ordinary man. It was a great come down.

CHAPTER XVIII.

THE RHINE AND COLOGNE.

"The river Rhine, it is well known,
Doth wash your city of Cologne;
But tell me, nymphs! what power divine
Shall henceforth wash the river Rhine?"

WE started on our sail down the Rhine in the morning, at 9:30 by steamer Deutscher Kaiser, arriving at Cologne at 5 P. M. It always seems to me to be "up" when I look at the map. I think the reason they say "down," is on account of the direction of the flow of the water. Since my return I have been frequently asked "which is the more beautiful, the Hudson or the Rhine?" I answer neither, for to my vision they are entirely unlike. The Rhine is historic, therein is its beauty, with its castles, old palaces and vineyards. It is a dirty stream, at some places very narrow, at no point so majestic in its water as our noble Hudson. I like the Hudson better because I drink it, now and then. Mary takes it in tea. On our trip down, she took Chablis and Seltzer, I was not mean enough to keep count of the number of bottles. She drank, however, all she ought in her feeble state of health. I took all kinds, as I wished to sample the brews of each noted place where wine is produced that I might know which was the best tonic for my patients, when I prescribe a light form of alcoholic stimulant.

The first place of note reached is Bingen, the home of the fellow who "lay dying in Algiers." Opposite, on the right hand shore, on the wooded height of Nierderwald is the great National monument, commemorating the restoration of the German Empire in 1870. It stands 740 feet above the river, and consists of a collossal statue of Germania 33 feet high, upon a pedestal 78 feet in height, adorned with historical and allegorical reliefs. Then Eltville, where a printing press was set up in 1465; then the Castle of Johannisberg, Geisenheim and Rüdesheim, both with their old castles, and noted for wines. Assmanshausen, famous for red wine, is at the end of the "great gorge of the Rhine," through which we were to sail. On the right the ruins of Ehrenfels and the Mausthurm, or Mouse Tower; then Lorch, Bacharach, with many little villages between. Longfellow says, as you will remember, in the Golden Legend,

> "At Bacharach on the Rhine,
> At Hocheim on the Main,
> And at Würzburg on the Stein,
> Grow the three best kinds of wine."

Caub, to the right. Oberwesel, to the left. St. Goar, on the left bank has, on the hill above Rheinfels, the most interesting ruin on the river.

It is of the 13th century. Then comes Welmich, above which is the castle of Thurnberg, or the "Mouse," built in the 14th century. Bornhofen, with the twin castles of Sternberg, and Liebenstein, Brauback, Rhense, Oberlaustein, passing the royal castle of Stolzenfols, on the left, to Coblence. Here the Moselle enters. Beyond is the long island of Niederwerth. We then come to Engers on the right, where as some antiquarians believe Cæsar made his second crossing of the Rhine. As we sail along, we pass Weissenthurm, with the old watch tower, A. D., 1379. On the height, to the right is a monument to the French General Hoche, who crossed here in 1797. Then Neuwied, and Andernach, with its ruined castle, ancient walls and lofty watch-tower. On the left Brohl, with the ruined castle of Hammerstein, built in the 10th century, and destroyed in 1660, by the Archbishop of Cologne. Linz, also on the right. Erpel, Remegen to Oberwinter, where ahead of you the view is the finest on the river. Königswinter, on the left, where is the old castle, what remains of it, a mere fragment, said to have been built by Roland, paladin of Charlemagne, who fell at the battle of Roncesvalles. Rolandseck comes next, after half an hour's sail. Last Bohn, twenty-one miles from Cologne.

COLOGNE.

We were doubly glad to reach Cologne, for here we found the first letters from home, bringing the gratifying intelligence that all were well. Mary was cured, after reading the first epistle, and I took a bottle of Cologne water on the kids.

Cologne, or Köln, was originally the chief town of the ancient Ubii, the Oppidum Ubiorum of Tacitus. It became known as Colonia Agrippina from A. D. 51, when Agrippina, who was born here while her father Germanicus held command in the district, induced her husband Claudius to send a colony of veteran soldiers to the place. It afterwards became the chief town of Germania Secunda, or Inferior. The Roman remains consist of what is called the Pfaffenporte, supposed to be the old Porta Claudia, and some fragments of the walls. Many statues, sarcophagi, mosaic pavements, &c., have been found in and about the city.

The Cathedral, the spires of which you see long before reaching the city, is the great glory. All things considered, it is the grandest Gothic church in the world. It was begun in 1248, but the choir was not consecrated until 1322. The spires, two of them, the tallest in the world, are 512 feet high. It contains much statuary and many paintings. The treasury guards a golden shrine of the 12th century, enclosing the bones of the Magi, brought from Constantinople to Milan by the Empress Helena, and afterwards transferred by Frederick Barbarossa to Cologne. The glass is fine, like some at Munich. Mary thinks it is the finest of all churches thus far seen. We visited the church of St. Ursula, 12th century, said to hold the bones of 11,000 virgins martyred by the Huns. (Prof. Andrew D. White in his recent work says they are mostly those of males and animals.) Bones are everywhere worked into the walls as mosaics, in every available place in the church. The skull of the saint, and a few of her chosen companions, are stowed away in the Golden Chamber, in the inside of gold and silver images. It was here I saw one of the vessels used at the marriage feast in Cana of Galilee. I put hand my into it, but the bridal party had not left a drop. A piece was broken out of the rim. While "doing" this church we saw a similar party. We were told by the guide the poor things had been there a couple of hours, kneeling and praying before the High Altar. I did not ask the innocent doves why they did it. Peace in the family, and with the prospective mother-in-law I presume was the object.

Into whatever gallery of paintings we went, we had been haunted by two pictures, Susanna at the bath, and St. Sebastian, the human pin-cushion. No matter where the gallery was, in church or palace, these two turned up. Mary was disgusted after she had seen two or three thousand Susannas, but I would have seen more. I looked her straight in the face, not as the Elders always were doing, through a crack, or half-opened door. Had I been there, I should have gone right in like a man, and offered to buy soap and towels, or help her wash. I got down on St. Seb'. Here I saw his bones and the arrow which killed him. I was thankful he was done for, and bade him, as I thought, an everlasting farewell. Not much; he and Susie turned up in the next museum. I'd like to get the two together, so as to make an end of the farce. I'll bet on Susie every time. Women like Mary would side with the old duffer Sebast'.

Less interesting churches are those of St. Gereon, with a nave as old as the 7th century, having skulls of the martyrs around under gilded arabesques; the Apostles' church, begun in 1200; St. Peter's, which has for an altar-piece the "Crucifixion of St. Peter." (You pay a fee to see it.) At No. 10, in the Sternengasse, Rubens is falsely said to have been born, and in the same house, (this is true,) Maria de Medici died in exile in 1642. St. Maria is built on the site of the Roman Capitol; then there are St. Martins, St. Andrews, where is the tomb of Albertus Magnus, and in the church of the Minorites is buried Duns Scotus, with a tombstone bearing the inscription, *Scotia me genuit, Anglica me suscepit, Gallia me docuit, Colonia me tenet.* The Rathhaus, or Hotel de Ville, or City Hall, was founded in the 13th century. The portico was added in the 16th. This latter has inscribed upon it, in Latin, expressions of gratitude to Julius Cæsar, Augustus, Agrippa, Constantine, Justinian, and the German Emperor Maximilian. The museum contains a valuable collection of antiquities. The monument to Frederick William III, is one of the best works of its class in Europe, It is in the Heumarkt. We rode over the fine bridges, saw the Zoological and Botanical Gardens, and much else of interest.

Mary enjoyed baths in Cologne water; she washed, drank and did all manner of things with it, even had tea made from it. They water the streets with it, and use it just as we do that of the Hudson river. For handkerchief and disinfecting purposes, we bought it in bottles. That which we purchased was "The Only Genuine Maria-Farina" We knew it was so, as it was obtained in a shop directly opposite the Cathedral. There are at least five hundred others, who claim the same genuiness, but they must be frauds. Any way, some one is not truthful. It may be Mary.

CHAPTER XIX.

AMSTERDAM. HAARLEM. THE HAGUE. SCHEVENINGEN.

IT was Sunday when we left Cologne for Amsterdam, "The Vulgar Venice." This was in accordance with our usual plan, Sunday and long rides being synonymous. We arrived early in the afternoon, which gave an opportunity of riding about the city. Holland had always been familiar in name, but not much of an acquaintance in fact. My forefathers came from this far-off land, and bequeathed to me many of their virtues but none of their vices. Mary's predecessors emigrated from Ireland. I need say nothing more. The country through which we passed was dotted everywhere with those giant windmills, too precious from tradition to be put aside for modern devices. We found a letter awaiting us from our daughter, and this added greatly to the health of mind and body we were enjoying.

AMSTERDAM is the commercial capital of Holland. It is situated on the influx of the Amstel, an arm of the Zuiderzee. It has a fine harbor and a lively trade, especially with its colonies. Diamond cutting is one of the great industries, which process Mary was anxious to see. I had an experience at Venice in the lace manufactories that taught me a lesson. She did not go. All of the houses are built on piles, which gave rise to the joke of Erasmus, that he knew "a city, the inhabitants of which dwelt on the tops of trees like rooks." As I walked about I could not help bringing to mind old Peter Stuyvesant with his wooden leg, and the New Amsterdam so far away. What changes have taken place since the old fellows sailed westward, seeking an extension of their trade in the New World! Everything is of interest here. The queer houses, the strange costumes, especially those worn by the people coming into town from neighboring burgs, the funeral processions and the "Schnapps." The language I could never seem to get hold of. It is a jargon to which my classic tongues and modern dialects give no aid. One must see Holand its inhabitants to obtain a real knowledge of what it and they are. We took in all we could, leaving much behind unseen, though wished for.

The Dam is the focus of business life. It is a large square and owes its name to the position on the west side of the old embankment with which the foundation of the old city is connected. The Dam is surrounded by the Exchange, the Royal Palace, the Nieuwe Kerk, and many private houses. It is the center from which the principal streets diverge, and where the tram-way cars gather. The Exchange is a handsome structure, built on 3469 piles, being completed in 1845. The Nieuwe Kerk, was erected in 1498, and is one of the most important in Holland. The monuments in the interior are all beautiful, and mostly dedicated to the memories of distinguished Admirals who fell in naval battles. The Royal Palace was begun in 1648. All the apartments are richly adorned with sculptures in white marble. The whole arrangement of both the exterior and interior carry us back to the days when a wealthy and powerful municipality congregated here.

The Kalverstraat, is one of the chief thoroughfares, and contains fine shops, restaurants and cafés. The University contains excellent portraits of eminent scholars. There is also a society of Arti et Amicitiæ, with pictures and scenes from the history of the Netherlands. In the Rembrandsplein is the statue of Rembrandt, and also his old house. Near is the house of Herr J. P. Six, containing a celebrated Gallery of Paintings. The Fodor Museum contains a valuable collection of paintings by ancient and modern masters, and for the study of the French school of the 19th century, is second to none save the Hertford collection in London.

We went through the Jewish Quarter, finding a marked contrast to the ideal Dutch cleanliness of the rest of the city. The Jews form one-tenth of the population and have ten Synagogues. The largest, that of the Portuguese Jews, is said to be in imitation of Solomon's Temple. The Ryks Museum is the finest and most charming of all the places we saw. It contains over three hundred rooms filled with the most exquisite pictures, porcelain, statues, weapons, engravings and works of art. The Dutch school is fully represented, Rembrandt especially. It is too large and grand to attempt a description of any part. Mary was particularly interested, as I see her catalogue is filled with marks of pictures, etc., that pleased her. Mary had grown by this time to be quite a connoisseur, (of course under my tutorage,) and could pick out a good painting when she saw it, and tell the reason why it had merit. She has quite a mind, the only trouble being in keeping it in the right direction, and upon subjects she can grasp.

Canals intersect the city in almost every part and wind in every direction. They are not so large as those in Venice, nor is there that beauty. They seem to have been made for short cuts to the harbor. You may drive along their banks, which are the streets of the town, beneath grand old trees, which give shade and shelter, making the thoroughfare cool, and producing a most picturesque appearance. It is with difficulty I restrain my pen from writing more of this quaint old city, its parks, gardens, museums, all that make up a part of the history of my native state. Even if you do not go to see it, read about it, as the story is enchanting. We would fain have lingered here, and gone into the little villages round about, to see what manner of men the descendents of the old Dutchmen were, their homes and mode of life, but our time was growing short and Mary was anxious to reach Paris in order to pick out that new bonnet. We did, however, take a day off, going to—

HAARLEM

that we might spend a few hours with an American lady who had won a bright Dutchman for a husband. It was an enjoyable visit, for I heard nothing but English spoken, and sat down to a real home dinner. Pie and bread, delicious cheese, common food I may say, such as I have at home. We had grown tired of the everlasting table d' hote, with the rolls that break your teeth, and the pastry that is made of nothing but sugar and foam. It was home-like, with a darling little boy who carried us back in memory to our children so far away. We feasted, not on the variety but on the quality of the viands. Then the talks, the recounting the "alls" that had happened since the departure of our friend from her native land. I tell you it was great. While sitting in the library of this delightful residence on Flora Park during the time my wife was arranging her toilet, I put out my hand to take a magazine, thinking to spend the moments in learning a bit of the Dutch language, when what should meet my astonished gaze but a newspaper from my own city. It was of recent date, and full of items which told me how the boys were getting on. I read every letter in that paper, advertisements and all. I found some of my friends had moved away, that my own son had changed his business, that some had died. Letters had been few and far between, but this little paper "filled a long felt want." My wife's name and my own were mentioned, and the public informed how we were getting on. This, no doubt, was learned from letters written to friends.

Haarlem is one of the cleanest cities of Holland, and has a special pride in the fact. It has large manufactories, well kept gardens and promenades, while tulips bloom everywhere, as they do all over the country. The Groote Kerk, erected in the 15th century is noted for its organ. In it is a monument to the memory of Conrad, the engineer who constructed the locks of Katwyk. There is a sounding board over the pulpit, and a cannon ball in the wall, the latter a reminiscence of the Spanish siege. Outside of the church, but really in it, is a fish-market. About the doors and along the side was the greatest collection of old used up traps I ever saw. Old locks, nails, pans, carpenter's tools, all lying on the ground and all for sale, a sort of out-door market for trash. In the market place is the bronze statue of Coster, the alleged inventor of printing. In the Town Hall, built in the 12th century, nearly opposite the church is the museum. It contains a small but valuable picture gallery, the only one where it is possible to become acquainted with the jovial Frans Hals, the greatest colorist of the Dutch painters next to Rembrandt.

Haarlem is adorned with parks, horticulture giving display to myriads of flowers, as hyacinths, tulips, crocuses and lilies. Some of these gardens, well repay a visit. Our friend guided us to every place that had enjoyment in it, and as the shadows fell, we returned to Amsterdam. From Amsterdam we went to—

THE HAGUE

once the hunting-seat of the Counts of Holland, whence its Dutch name 'S Graven Hage, or den Haag (i. e. "the Count's enclosure," or "hedge." It has been for centuries the favorite residence of the Dutch princes. It possesses many broad and handsome streets, lofty and substantial houses, spacious and imposing squares. While there are many important and beautiful public buildings, the chief attraction is the Picture Gallery, (Koninklyle Kabinet van Schilderyen) founded by the princes of the House of Orange. Rembrandt and Potter are the heroes of the collection. The catalogue now numbers upward of four hundred and fifty paintings, the greatest number belonging to the Dutch school. The pictures which attract the most attention are, Rembrandt's celebrated School of Anatomy, and Potter's Bull. The former called back my days of medical college life, making me wish I were a boy again. It was painted for the Amsterdam Guild of Surgeons in 1632 and intended to be hung in the Dissecting Room. It is said to be "the truest and most life like representation of the working intellect ever produced." The other, the far-famed Bull of Paul Potter, is the most popular picture in the collection. The fly on the animal causing many ludicrous mistakes, as not a few attempt to brush it off. Many statues adorn the city. In the Plein is that of Prince William I, in bronze. In the Buttenhof, the bronze statue of William II. In front of the Royal Palace, built in the time of Stadtholder, William III, is the equestrian statue of Prince William I, of Orange.

The Town Hall, Municipal Museum and Library contain statuary and paintings with other objects of art, the latter a valuable collection of coins, medals and gems. In the center of Willems Park, stands the National Monument, unveiled in 1869, to commemorate the restoration of Dutch Independence in 1813, and the return of William of Orange, who afterward became King. The principal churches are the Groote Kerk, and the Nieuwe Kerk. There are Zoölogical and Botanical gardens, and many houses and residences of men whose ancestors lived a life of virtue and died distinguished. An attractive spot, not to be missed in a visit to The Hague, is the "House in the Wood," the Huisten Bosh, a royal villa, erected in 1647 for the Princess Amalia of Solms, the widow of Henry of Orange. The interior contains many pictures, the best being in the dining-room, the latter having imitations of bas-reliefs, producing a perfect illusion.

Nearly all the commoner children wear wooden shoes (sabots) as do the laboring men and women. No where did we see so many in use. Though they look clumsy, they appear to be worn with as much ease and comfort as their leathern brothers. I thought of buying a pair for Mary, as they are cheaper than those she has made to order, and I think would last as long and do more service. I could hear her coming if I were alone with a pretty girl. This would save embarrassment. While here I did a little shopping for Mary. Buttons will come off, and garments rip and tear. Our clothing began to show the effects of use, but we were trying to keep them together, and appear decent until we arrived in Paris, where that bonnet was to be purchased, and where we also expected to add to our supply of raiment. I got what Mary wanted, and at the same time saw a good deal of the town, as I lost my way.

SCHEVENINGEN, a few miles from The Hague, is among the most noted bathing resorts on the continent, and the most expensive. It is frequented by about 20,000 visitors annually, including ourselves. The bathing boxes, or baskets, are curious looking affairs, which stand all over the beach, one for each bather. We did not bathe, for many reasons. One of which was, that I preferred to wait till I reached Paris, where I understood beautiful young ladies assist in the operation. Mary did not know this, but accepted my excuses for not going into the water.

As we were seated in the carriage on leaving The Hague, just about to start for the station, one of the servants of the hotel opened the carriage door, and informed me I had forgotten to remember him. His cheek was so angelic, I put my hand into my pocket and gave him a franc. I was not forgotten, in this respect at least, no matter where I went.

CHAPTER XX.

ANTWERP.

"Smiling at us with its fair towers."

FROM The Hague we left for Antwerp, passing through Rotterdam where we had intended stopping, but that Paris bonnet broke up more plans and good intentions than anything I ever met, unless it is old age.

Antwerp is the most interesting town in Belgium, the principal arsenal of the kingdom, and one of the strongest fortresses in Europe. Here Rubens was born. Antwerp is true to art, and looks just like its pictures. Even the dread of having to open your trunk for inspection by the Custom Officers does not mar the pleasure of seeing it. The officials were very lenient, and let everything pass. I think it was because the inspector on looking at our trunk, concluded, with rare judgment, the owners of such an outfit could not afford to smuggle anything. There is an old saying that "Brussels rejoices in noble men, Antwerp in money, Louvain in learned men, and Mechlin in fools, for the people go to bed at 7 o'clock." This inspector did not come from Mechlin.

The fascinating influence of Rubens cannot be appreciated without a visit to this delightful city, where his finest works are preserved. Our hotel was at the side of the Cathedral, whither we wended our way as soon as we had eaten luncheon. It is the largest and most beautiful Gothic church in the Netherlands. It was begun in 1352, and does not as yet appear completed. In 1566 it was seriously damaged by puritanical zealots, and again by fire and the French Republicans. The interior is grand and impressive, the vaulting being supported by 125 pillars. Here are the two celebrated paintings by Rubens. "The Descent from the Cross," and "The Elevation of the Cross." The former is what is called a "winged" picture, that is, shut up in a kind of box, ostensibly to keep the dust from soiling it, but really to get a fee for showing it. The other is covered by a curtain for the same reason. Over the high altar is his "Assumption," said to have been painted in sixteen days. In one of the chapels is the "Resurrection," painted for his friend the printer Moretus. Plantin's tomb is another, bearing an inscription on the stone by Justus Lipsius. There are a lot more pictures and stone saints, candles and other bric-a-brac, I have not time to describe. If the Cathedral lacks in anything, it makes up the loss in noise. It has a chime of ninety-nine bells, very different in the quality of tone from those spoken of in the church at home. Near the tower outside the church is the famous well, with its iron canopy, wrought by Quentin Matsys, the blacksmith artist. It is a love story, too long to be written here. Matsys is buried close beside the tower, and his tombstone, which has been removed to the museum, says in curious old Latin, "Love converted an ironsmith into an Apelles."

Things are all together in Antwerp. You are not obliged to walk or ride miles to see the different objects of interest. This saves a lot of trouble and a large waste of money. In front of the Cathedral is the Place Verte, formerly a churchyard, and adorned with a statue of Rubens in bronze. It seems not only to be the market-place and flower-mart, but the abode of more dogs than any other spot in the world. The ringing of the bells, and the barking of the dogs, got me out of bed earlier than I usually rise when on a tour for health. Here too are the Postoffice, the street car center, the best cafés and stores. It is the center of the city's life. In the square is an immense iron fountain representing Silvius Brabo throwing the giant Antigon's hand into the Scheldt. There is a legend about this, as well as about everything in Antwerp, but you must read them up in some other book.

Most of the houses in the Grand Place are "Guild Houses," formerly occupied by the different corporations, and dating from the 16th and 17th centuries, the coopers, tailors, carpenters, and others. The Hotel de Ville is situated here, containing more interesting pictures. I was shown through it by a mighty pretty girl. Mary was at the hotel, resting. A few steps from the City Hall is the Vielle Boucherie, or old fish-market. Farther on is a statue in marble of Van Dyck. Near is the Academie des Beaux Arts. Then comes the Musee Kums with one hundred and seventy paintings. Still farther the Capuchin Church, erected in 1589, containing two valuable pictures, one by Van Dyck, the other by Rubens. Of course it has others. A little beyond, is the church of St. Augustine, erected in 1615, also having paintings by Rubens. Near the Rue National is the Platin-Moretus Monument, filled with interesting relics of these ancient painters, copies of their work, presses, plates, proof reading stalls with the names of the readers above them, everything belonging to these wonderful men. The business was started in the house of Christopher Platin in 1549.

The Church of St. Jacques, built near the end of the 15th century, contains the tomb of Rubens, and is next to the Cathedral in magnificence, containing more sumptuous monuments and decorations. St Andrew's Church is, like all the others, stone saints and pictures. It was built, they say, in 1514 and looks as if it had been. St. George is another. The Museum is a fine one. To write about all the pictures and articles in it, would only be to rewrite the catalogue. You may buy one for two or three francs, so I am not going to waste time over it. Van Dyck's and Ruben's and a lot of other celebrated masters are all over the city, that is, their paintings, and you get your money's worth in seeing them.

One of the curious churches is that of St. Paul, built in 1540. It contains Ruben's "Scourging of Christ." The garden is the interesting place. Down in a cave are representations in stone of heaven and the other place, of Christ on the cross, and lying in the tomb, happy looking angels, and unfortunate gentlemen behind bars amid flames, begging for water, as they had no use for money. Then there is Mount Calvary, with saints and all the Apostles in stone. Above, that is outside in the garden, are more saints and apostles. If the garden were larger there would be more, but the artists have done well with what they had, in things terrestrial and celestial. You cannot expect a man to do much in representing heaven and earth and the bad place within a few square feet. Near the Cathedral lies the former Jesuit Church, built in 1614. It has a handsome facade and bell-tower.

There are other parks, churches, and monuments, some of which we did not see, and if we had, are too numerous to describe in this already too long chapter. My pen tempts me to say something concerning the elegant wharves, but I forbear. It was Mary's birthday while here. I gave her a good dinner, one of my old Life Insurance Policies, and promised her a new bonnet when we reached Paris. I think that was doing well.

CHAPTER XXI.
BRUSSELS.

EVER since our return from Europe we have been asked "Did you see the Wiertz Museum?" I am happy to say we did not. It was not because we did not care to do so, but because it rained. I am glad it did rain, for it has given those who have seen it an opportunity to tell us how much we missed. If we had visited it, they would have said nothing about it. It is the same way with pictures. If any one asks me if I saw so and so, I tell them yes, for in the millions I did see, there was small chance of my missing it, and I do not feel I have told an untruth. Mary tries to be more exact, going to her Baedeker or catalogue to see if it is marked in the proper place. By the time she has found out, the questioner has forgotten all about the question. My time is worth money, and I cannot waste it on such trifles. I have read it up, however, in the guide book, and do not think we have lost such an awful lot. We shall not make a special trip to see it. We saw everything else.

Brussels is the capital of Belgium, and the residence of the Royal Family. It is situated nearly in the center of the kingdom on the river Senne. The principal attractions are the Place Royale, laid out in 1778, where is the chief traffic of the city. Here is the Church of St. Jacques sur Caudenberg built in 1776. In front of the church is the statue of Godfrey de Bouillon, the hero of the first Crusade. Opposite is Montagne de la Cour street, which though steep, has a stream of vehicles constantly passing through it. Here too are some fine shops. Not far off on another street is the Palace of the Comte de Flandre, to which we could not obtain admission. I do not think he recognized my card, The Palais Royal contains some ancient and modern pictures. A flag hoisted at the palace announces the King is at home. It was not up while we were there, or we should have called. Near the Royal Palace is the Palais des Academies, also called the Ducal Palace, formerly that of the Prince of Orange. It is occupied by societies of medicine, beaux-arts, and letters. In the garden about it are statues of Quetelet, the Astronomer, a Victor in bronze, Cain, a Discus-thrower, and a group of Cupid and Psyche. The Palais de la Nation is in the Rue de la Loi. It was erected in 1779. Around about are government buildings.

The Colonne du Congres is a fine monument erected to commemorate the Congress of 1831. It is 147 feet in height, and surmounted by a figure of the King in bronze 13 feet in height. Other figures in relief are about it. The Cathedral (Ste. Gudule et St. Michel) is a fine Gothic structure, built in 1220. It contains much of interest in the way of stained glass, portraits in glass, monuments and carved work. Opposite the Cathedral is the National Bank. The Royal Library contains a vast number of ancient autographs, books, playing-cards and the like. The Musee Moderne contains over two hundred and twenty paintings, sculptures, and forty water colors and drawings displayed in eight rooms. In the upper town are the churches of Notre Dame des Victoires and the monument to Counts Egmont and Hoorn. As they were bad men they were executed. Later it was found a mistake had been made, so to offset the deed and make it right with some one, this monument was set up.

Here are the palace of the Duc d'Arenberg, erected in 1548, containing a small picture gallery, The Conservatory of Music, and the magnificent Palais de Justice. This is the largest building in the world, St. Peter's at Rome not excepted. It is a mass of sculptured and polished marble, surmounted by a tower 400 feet high. In the rotunda are colossal figures of Justice, Law, Strength and Clemency. The flights of steps ascending to the vestibule are adorned with immense statues of Demosthenes and Lycurgus, Cicero and Domitius Ulpian. The interior includes twenty-seven large court rooms, two hundred and forty-five other apartments, and eight open courts. The Waiting Room is in the center, under the dome, which has an interior height of 320 feet. It is the most magnificent building in itself I ever saw. In the lower part of the town, back of the Hotel de Ville, is the Manikin Fountain. It has quite a history. Mary did not not like it. I brought home a little pewter imitation, so as not to forget it.

The Grande Place is said to be one of the finest mediæval squares in existence. In 1568, twenty-five nobles were beheaded here, for what, I do not remember. The mistake will be found out later, and all will get monuments. The Hotel de Ville, is one of the noblest and most beautiful buildings in Belgium. There are a lot of empty niches on the facade, perhaps intended for monuments to those executed nobles. Opposite the Hotel de Ville is the Halle au Pain, better known as the House of the King. It was formerly the seat of the government authorities. There was an earlier building on the present site, said to have been occupied by Pope Innocent II, and King Bernard. Then there are the churches of Notre Dame de la Chapelle, the Musee Commercial, the Guild Houses, the Galerie St. Hubert, markets, theaters, exchanges, beautiful streets, promenades and parks too numerous to mention. The Martyrs' Monument, erected in 1838 to the memory of the Belgians (445) who fell in 1830 in the war against the Dutch, is one of the finest we saw in the city.

We did not go to the Zoölogical gardens, as we were tired of seeing half-fed animals. They all look alike, but please the small boy. They may go. Mary is lion enough for me and does not appear starved.

One thing I saw astonished me. It was a Belgian pie. Thirty inches across the top, and two inches thick, large enough for a Thanksgiving dinner to all your next of kin. I did not eat one. Mary did, but bought it with her own money. She had recovered entirely from the cold taken at Berlin. It was so wet and rainy, we did not go over to the field of Waterloo. I had been on enough battle fields, being married, and did not care to spend money for relics I knew were not genuine. Mary and I had no fight over the matter, I giving in as usual.

There was a blamed pretty chambermaid at the hotel I wanted Mary to engage for our home in America. She declined on the ground she did not speak French well enough to bother with her. I do not think this was the real reason she had in mind. Of course Mary bought more lace, as she had heard it was well made in this city. It looked as moth eaten as any she has. I bought——, well never mind.

CHAPTER XXII.

PARIS. VERSAILLES.

"Where Love reigns, disturbing Jealousy."

Paris takes five letters only to spell it, and an entire encyclopedia to describe it. The difference is so great between the two, I shall not attempt it. Mary and I took in all we could during the day, I taking in more at night, when it was not prudent for her to be out. I do not wonder Mary prefers being buried here, rather than at Pisa. I certainly should, and have the resurrection the next morning. Paris is so near New York, it would be a waste of ink to speak of its architectural and art beauties. We read of them almost daily, and see them in print, taken like shadows, but not so departing. Its joys, its pleasures, its abandon, all that goes to make up its gay and butterfly life, must be met in person, to know what they are. No words can convey the faintest idea.

The ride over had not been so pleasing as we anticipated, the country having grown more familiar by reason of travel through Holland and Belgium. It was much the same, topographically. There was a long detention in the Custom House after our arrival late in the afternoon, due either to the number of packages to be examined, or the thoroughness with which it was done. Ours passed quickly, no doubt due to the wisdom of the Inspectors, a sort of insight into our little trunk and bags. It was late after dinner, so save a short stroll, we retired early, in order to be prepared for the pleasures of the morrow. The morrow being Sunday, we rode about the city, into the Bois de Bologne, Champs Elysees, Champs de Mars, where is the Eiffel Tower, through the principal streets and Boulevards till we were tired. Late in the afternoon we strolled into the Louvre, more to get an idea of what was to be seen than to see. We visited it daily, and before we left had viewed all its treasures of art, from the Immaculate Conception to the Venus de Milo. Words cannot describe what is here gathered.

This same evening (Sunday) I, not being able to understand preaching in the French language, and as it was also long after the hours of service, went down into the Latin Quarter to call on Trilby. Her mother told me she had gone to a dance. This I thought strange, and as I never had done it on Sunday, regarding such a performance as wrong, forthwith went in search of her to bring her home. I went to the place where the ball was being held, to hunt her up. When I arrived, I found several hundreds of ladies and gentlemen had accepted invitations for a good time. It was what is called "The Student's Ball," a very unceremonious affair, taking place regularly twice a week, on Thursday and Sunday evenings. When I am in Paris, I do as the Parisians do, so joined the choir and went in for what was to be had. In Paris, Sunday comes next month, so I violated no moral law. Every one was glad to see me and made me feel much at my ease. The young ladies were particularly attentive, asking me to invite them to a glass of wine. I did, as I believed it to be the proper thing to do under the circumstances, which were novel, and good practice for the next time. I never knew exactly how it occurred, by accident I presume, but one of the ladies kicked off my hat. This taught me if I were to keep up with the procession while here, I must assume a virtue if I had it not, so the following day I shaved off my beard, including the two or three grey hairs, and came out a comparatively young looking man. As the hat had become rather rusty after so much exposure to sea and travel, I decided to change it for one better adapted to my now younger years. I did so without informing Mary. It was a mistake. As the weather was warm, I judged a light straw would be the *fromage*, (as we say in French) so bought what I thought became my style of form and beauty. I did this on my own responsibility, and appeared before her with the purchase on my head. Words fail to express her disapproval, I suppose she would say "disgust." I thought it mighty fine, and felt if I could bring it home, it would be the admiration, if not the envy of my male friends. It was only a simple white straw hat, with the brim dyed a beautiful blue on the underside, and around the crown a ribbon of white and red silk. What could be more simple? Mary had interviewed the monument of art but a few seconds, when in language similar to that used on the ship when I brought back the change from the smoke-room, ordered me to exchange it. I did so at the cost of two francs to boot. I have always been sorry I did, but it is better to make such mistakes, than to have Mary down on you. The hat, I must say, gave her a motherly appearance when we were together, producing a boyish look in me, the very thing I desired. Nearly all, (there were few exceptions) of my purchases thereafter, were made through her advice. They cost more in the end, but avoided a row. My sister, her husband and daughter, met us while here, having come up from Genoa through Switzerland. My sister and niece, with Mary, bought that bonnet so frequently spoken of, but no consultation was held with me as to my opinion on so gigantic a transaction. You will readily see the difference.

We were fortunate enough to find Opera going on. That bonnet and the rest of us went, and we had a box, too, more for the bonnet than for anything else. It gave us an opportunity to see the interior of the Grand Opera House lighted, its magnificent staircase, and Foyer. The opera was Faust. No great artists, in the role, but there were angels in the ballet. This latter is said to be the finest in the world. I regret not having seen the others for the purpose of comparison. Nevertheless it was by far the most gorgeous spectacle of the kind I had ever witnessed, reminding me of the days of "Black Crook" when that celebrated play made its first appearance in New York, when Bonfanti and Sangalli astonished the city by their grace of action and pose.

I well remember the day that bonnet arrived. It was delivered by a young lady and a small dog. We had two rooms, (a double apartment) adjoining. Mary had the better, of course, and to this, the aforesaid young lady with the precious bundle came. That was all proper enough and I found no fault. Now I had the larger looking-glass. When the darling was taken from the box, and handed to my wife, I suggested that she and the jewel should go into my quarters to see if it was on straight, leaving the young lady with me, that I might see if were not possible to get two francs reduction in the price to make up for the loss on my hat. Would she do it? Not much. I have always had a suspicion she thought I was in for a deal for another hat for myself, but there is no knowing a woman's thoughts, they may have been entirely different. As to the bonnet, I never had a great opinion of it. I saw no difference between those she buys at home, except in price. That of this Parisian affair was greater.

Our guide was a young fellow about my age who became very much attached to us, or at least to me. One evening he took me to the "Moline Rouge," a queer kind of church, but the congregation was large and the music fine. While walking about, some pretty young ladies addressed him in Spanish. Now as he spoke English but little better than I spoke French, I found another tie between us. We gave up our *patois*, and thereafter used Castillian only. Through this brotherhood I saw many things I might otherwise have missed. I was glad I knew Spanish. While we were in Paris we happened to strike some of the party of "The Ancient and Honorable Artillery," who had come over from Boston to London on an excursion of some sort, and were now taking in the sights of the gay capital. Among the number were a clergyman and his most intimate friend, perhaps a deacon, or elder in his church, perhaps neither. One night my friend the guide, asked me if I would not like to take some one with me for a stroll. The elder (?) and I had grown quite intimate, so I told him I had an opportunity of seeing some of the "Delights," and asked him to be my guest. He told me he could not go, unless his friend the clergyman went with him, as he had promised the clergyman's wife to keep an eye on him while here. I said that was perfectly agreeable. The minister however, refused, so neither went. It was better in the end. What reasons the reverend gentleman gave as an excuse, are unknown to me, but I surmise. I think it likely he feared that on some occasion the friendship might be broken, and one of the two give the other away. Why should he? If it is worth the while to build up a character, what does it amount to if it will not come to the rescue when occasion demands? My character took me through. Ask Mary.

There are some wonderful things to be seen in Paris, if you can get on to them. I would like to tell all about them, but have not room in the present volume. I may write an appendix. Mary did a good deal of sight-seeing in the Maisons du Louvre, and the Bon Marche. While she was viewing these grand stores, I was visiting as my fancy dictated. It feels good to be free now and then. I struck one store where photographs were sold, not only on cards, but on boxes, fans, pipes, cigar cases and any other handy thing for ornament, or personal use. Mary was with me at the time, but objected to my buying what pleased my fancy. I therefore resolved to go to it again the next day to make such purchases of views as I desired, but never could find the place. Mary said she could, but would not. I think the concern burned up in the night, for it mysteriously disappeared from my ability ever to discover it. She never lost the bonnet shop. Had she done so, and I had known where it was I would have told her.

The only rascally piece of business committed while on our outing was by Mary. The day I ascended the Eiffel Tower, she refused to go, fearing the height (nearly 1000 feet) would make her dizzy. So while I mounted, she hired a chair from an old woman, and on my return did not pay for its use. Ten centimes, two cents of our money, is too small an amount out of which to beat a person, and were I she, would never put my face in the town again. When I go over alone I shall pay the bill with interest. I enjoy a clear conscience. We visited many of the hospitals, the morgue (behind the church of Notre Dame) in which were two bodies. In Notre Dame we saw the recent grave of Pasteur, covered with flowers. The monument has not as yet been erected. We spent an afternoon in the cemetery of Pere Lachaise. Here a guide took us to all tombs of interest. It is a poorly kept plot, the graves being rented for a longer or shorter term of years, or in perpetuity. Of course we saw that of Abelard and Heloise. I guess Mark Twain tells the truth about the parties, or what is left of them. To me there was a vast deal of professional interest in the tombs of the great French Surgeons and Physicians, as Amusat, Claude Bernard, Bichat, Dupuytren, Nelaton and a host of others. Here, in the sweetest rest are many of the great musical composers, Auber, Cherubini, Pleyel, and their peers. Marshalls of the Empire under Napoleon, from Ney to Suchet, Presidents, Revolutionists, Novelists, Painters, men and women who have crowned kings and wrecked Empires. It is a wonderful spot, this "God's Acre." Sarah Bernhardt has her tomb already erected, and on each visit to the capital, daily places flowers upon it with her own hands. Lafayette is not buried here, but in the little cemetery of Picus in a street of the same name. The great Actress Rachel lies in the Israelite cemetery adjoining Pere Lachaise, with other noted Hebrews. We saw the most interesting.

We rode over to VERSAILLES with our guide. Here again is a book by itself. After all nothing can be told of Paris, it must be seen. Like Rome it has a history, which can only be truly read and understood by seeing it as it is. We used up considerable small change in one way or another, Mary buying gloves, laces and traps such as a man knows nothing about. I tried to buy photographs, but you know my experience.

CHAPTER XXIII.

LONDON.

KEW. HAMPTON COURT. WINDSOR. ETON.

WE went over to London by the way of Calais and Dover. The day was warm and the channel passage smooth, though some on board were made ill. It was a welcome sound to hear again all speech about you in a tongue that gave no chance of misinterpretation. The ride from Dover to London was charming. Everywhere about were cultivated farms, blooming gardens, comfortable homes. We saw none of that "Pauper Labor" politicians talk so much about during election campaigns either here, or elsewhere, unless it was in Italy, where other circumstances govern, as the Church, a depreciated currency, etc.

LONDON, I must talk of as I did of Paris. I cannot describe the many places of interest we visited, it is too big. I did not take a fancy to it, though there may have been a reasonable cause. We went to one of those family temperance hotels, kept by a friend of a friend of mine. You could get nothing to drink with your dinner, and were locked out of the house if not at home by midnight. It was clean, delightfully situated, just the place for women and retired clergymen, In the words of Artemus Ward "for those who like it, it is just such a place as such people like." It was however to me, personally, a great change, coming from the gay capitals of the Continent, with their fine hotels, and all the freedom you desired. Mary liked it, "it was so quiet." Situated at the side of the British Museum, near Holborn street, it is a convenient point from which to start for all places. The meals did not suit us. At breakfast the coffee was mixed, as if we were children. I never drink milk in mine, but here could not get it otherwise. Then again, the bread was passed from one boarder to another and he, or she, cut off a piece the size desired, by holding onto the body of the loaf. Who knew where their hands had been last? Some one, without doubt, eventually swallowed the microbes which came off the loaf. You are obliged to "eat your peck of dirt" during your life-time I know, but you take it with less disgust when you are not aware of its presence, than when you see it laid on. After the first meal we took all others elsewhere. We still continued to breakfast here, as going out early in the morning was most inconvenient for Mary, but I gave up coffee and bread. Mary stuck to tea and somehow or other got some rolls. The closing of the doors at 12 P. M. was an affliction, and broke up many a good time. I can never forgive them for causing me to leave the finest display of living pictures I ever saw on the stage. It brought me other anxieties, but was a comfort to Mary.

Fortunately for us, two old friends were residing in the city, both playmates of mine in younger days. One a chemist of renown, whose fame grows as his life lengthens and the results of his labor are given to the world. The other, an artist, whose works adorn the National Gallery in London, and other galleries in the great cities of Europe, and who in loving remembrance of our boyhood had painted for me a little picture of a bit of English landscape, embodying in it all the genius and art which have won for him so many laurels. These two made London life endurable. The city itself is old, black, and without private beauty. The palaces, courts, public buildings, abbeys, churches and monuments are grand, not only in structure, but in their histories. The best way to see London, is from the top of a 'bus. This I did as often as I could get away from Mary, riding into all parts of the city, accompanied by my friend the chemist. Together, Mary and I did well with the "Hansoms," a two-wheel sort of cab, which needs no description.

Of all places, Westminster Abbey was the spot I most desired to visit, as being "the only National place of Sepulchre in the world." I wished to see the spot which contained the remains of Charles Darwin, the man who did so much to remove the scales from the eyes of dogmatic theology, and made religion more precious and men happier, and of whom some one, paraphrasing the scripture says, "God said, let Darwin be, and there was light." I desired to stand by the tomb of Major Andre, of whom my great-grandfather took charge, by order of Gen. Washington, the night before his execution. My great-grandfather, I think was a witness to Andre's will. He saw him draw the portrait of himself which is now in Trumball Gallery in Yale College, and commanded the guard which hung him the next morning. My great-grandfather was a captain on Gen. Washington's staff, and these facts have been often told me by his son, my grandfather. On the tomb was a little bunch of withered flowers, tied with a white ribbon, having a card attached on which were written these words: "From an English woman in America, to be placed on Major Andre's monument in Westminister Abbey." I thought well of the woman for her loyalty, as well as of the patriotism of my great-grandfather who hung him. The intentions of both were good. I can say nothing else here of the Abbey, it is so immense, so full of history, so awe-inspiring. Book after book has been written concerning it, yet the half has not been told. The same may be said of St. Paul's and of the Tower. If but a single day is to be spent in London, these three places should be visited, if nothing else.

Of the Tower and of St. Paul's I must say a few words. The Tower is the most interesting spot in England. It was once an ancient fortress and gloomy prison, surrounded by a moat. At first a royal palace, it is best known as a prison. Within is a collection of armor, ancient and modern, the Crown Jewels, magnificent to be sure, but not in my opinion equal to those in the treasury at Vienna. The Koh-i-Noor was absent, they probably having heard of Mary's coming, and her action toward the old woman in Paris. Here in the White Tower are the axe which had brought death to so many, and the block with the marks of the blade upon it. Outside and in different parts of the building are stationed the quaintly attired "Beef Eaters," old soldiers who had been discharged after meritorious service. Each of the twelve towers making up "The Tower" has an indissoluble history, connected with it, with marked and painful memories. In the Bloody Tower the sons of Edward IV were murdered. In the Bell Tower the Princess Elizabeth was confined by her sister Queen Mary. Lady Jane Grey is said to have been imprisoned in the Brick Tower, Lord Dudley in Beauchamp Tower. In the Bowyer Tower the Duke of Clarence, brother of Edward IV, is popularly supposed to have been drowned in a cask of beer, and Henry VI is believed to have been murdered in Record Tower. The Beauchamp Tower was to us the most interesting of all. Here upon the walls are the inscriptions made by the hands of those who died upon the scaffold, and of those who languished within its cells. These inscriptions were the more interesting, in as much as we knew they constituted the employment by which their unfortunate authors beguiled the tedious hours of their dreary captivity, or perhaps, strove to drown the remembrance that in a few short hours they must prepare to meet an untimely end.

Near by is the Chapel of St Peter ad Vincula. Within it we saw the graves of Sir Thomas More, Queen Anne Boleyn, the Earl of Essex, Catherine Howard, Lord Seymour, Lord Somerset, Lady Jane Grey, and her husband Lord Dudley and others known to fame and history. Those beheaded in the Tower itself, were Anne Boleyn, Catherine Howard, the Countess of Salesbury, Lady Jane Grey and the Earl of Essex. The other prisoners were executed on Tower Hill. Of this little chapel, Macaulay says: "In truth there is no sadder place on earth—death is here associated—with what ever is darkest in human nature and in human destiny, with the savage triumph of implacable enemies, with the inconstancy, the ingratitude, the cowardice of friends, with all the miseries of fallen greatness and of blighted fame." After looking at the old armor in the White Tower, one of the attendants told me there was but a single American gun in the establishment, and asked if we would like to see it. Of course we said yes. He brought forth from behind an old counter, a revolutionary flint lock, marked U. S. I gave him a tip for showing it, (that was what he was after) and told him to keep it securely as it was "the only one the English would ever get." He smiled.

St. Paul's Cathedral resembles St. Peter's at Rome, but is vastly smaller. In front is a statue of Queen Anne, with England, France, Ireland and America at her feet. The interior strikes one as bare and dark, but is imposing from the beauty of the vastness of its proportions. It is a kind of National Temple of Fame. On the main floor are monuments to Wellington, Gordon, Napier, Dr. Samuel Johnson and other distinguished dead. Below in the Crypt, stands the polished granite sarcophagus of Wellington, and the marble one of Nelson. At the end are the hearse and trappings used at the funeral of the "Iron Duke." Many other memorials of distinguished men are also here.

Another object of interest was the "Old Curiosity Shop." We looked into it, and thought of "Poor Little Nell." So day after day we kept visiting, in the evening taking a cup of tea at the rooms of the chemist, or supping with the artist and his charming wife, then to some place of amusement, then to Holborn Restaurant, Frascati's or the "Old Cheshire Cheese." This latter is the place or inn so often frequented by Sam

Johnson, Goldsmith and Dickens. We read the inscriptions over the seats in which they once sat, and tried to fill their vacant places. It was from here, while Goldsmith's land-lady was pressing him within doors and the bailiff without, that Dr. Johnson took the manuscript of the "Vicar of Wakefield" and sold it for three hundred dollars to James Newberry, returning with the money to set Goldsmith free. Over the bench so often occupied by Johnson, engraved on a brass plate, is the following inscription from Boswell's Life of the Old Critic: "There is nothing which has yet been contrived by man, by which so much happiness is produced as by a good tavern or inn." He's right. Here is "ye old corner, ye old fire place, ye old stair way," and a portrait of "ye old waiter." We saw the beer mugs of these old giants of the literary world, and other memorials of their days. We drank beer and ate toasted cheese, smoked the long "Church Wardens" pipe as did they, and brought them home to the hotel unbroken, evidence that we were sober. I even brought mine to America, and still have it in perfect preservation. I also bought one of the old mugs. Call upon me, and you shall have a draught from its interior. A short time before we left for home, one of the practitioners of my city came to our Asylum with his wife and little son. Together we enjoyed a few days in the Hospitals and about town.

Mary and I took a drive in Hyde Park. This is no simple matter. You are not allowed to go in a "Hansom" or in any ordinary carriage. You must put on your best "bib and tucker," have a swell turn-out, a driver in livery, with a "bug" on his hat, and all the trimmings of greatness. We did it, inviting our friend the chemist to accompany us. None of us had been surrounded by so much style since we were baptized. It is a beautiful place, filled with elegant carriages, their occpants dressed in the height of fashion, ladies and gentlemen on horse back, and a world of nobility about. We saw several Royal Nibs. It is here the magnificent Albert Memorial is located.

Another spot I enjoyed visiting was the Charter House so connected with Thackeray's fictitious Col. Newcomb. Perhaps the fact that it was built (in 1371) over the site of a burying ground for persons dying of the plague, lent an additional charm.

We visited KEW GARDEN and HAMPTON COURT on Sunday as is so frequently done, sailing up the Thames on one of the peculiar little steamers. I see by Mary's diary much is marked as being seen. The palace is the largest (royal) one in Great Britain. You will remember it was built in 1515 by Cardinal Wolsey, and afterwards presented by him to Henry VIII. We did not venture into the Maze, though we saw all that was worth seeing from Trophy Gate to the Lion Gate.

While Mary went shopping at "The Universal Provider's," the chemist and I took a day off to to see what was in Windsor and Eton.

WINDSOR is more like a castle than any I had seen. It looks as do the pictures in "Jack the Giant Killer," high up, great walls about and turrets towering in the air. We engaged as a guide an old man who had lived here all his life, and who said he was present at the coronation of Queen Victoria. He took us everywhere, seeming to have a sort of right of way. The place is filled with monuments and pictures, chapels and prisons. The Albert Chapel contains the sarcophagi of the Prince Consort, the Duke of Albany, and the Duke of Clarence, eldest son of the present Prince of Wales. I went through the Royal stables, with some Duke or Prince. He may, however, have been only the stableman, but he looked his station and was not below or above, taking a shilling for the trouble.

ETON is within easy walk of Windsor, so over the bridge we went. It was vacation time, still we had a good look within and without. Of course while in London we dropped into Mme. Tassaud's Wax Work Show. We found a big crowd, and much to commend as well as much to dissatisfy. President Cleveland's wax figure, for instance. It was first, too short, second, too thin, looking as if the man weighed no more than 150 pounds; third, he was dressed in a second-hand suit, no two articles of which came from the same store. He looked a curiosity as I suppose the English people regarded him. But a short time before he had issued his celebrated message relative to the Venezuela matter. It was true, he was not all there, quite a little of him being left over, not many thousand miles away. We also saw the "greatest curiosity in the world," namely "the blade of the Guillotine which cut off the heads of 22,000 persons during the French Revolution."

The day I returned from Windsor I found Mary happy. She had been to Whiteley's and elsewhere, bought a trunk and enough to fill it, after my new overcoats had been put in. She was also financially broke. They tell an amusing story of this Whiteley, which runs somewhat as follows: He (Whiteley) says there is no article on earth he cannot supply on demand. A party of gentlemen laid a wager they could stump him, so ordered a second-hand coffin to be sent to a certain address, at a certain hour that night. He agreed to do it. When the time arrived, a ring at the door announced the arrival of the goods, accompanied by a note from Mr. Whiteley, saying he could "not furnish a second-hand article but the one sent is a misfit, and think it may answer the purpose." Every one who knows Whiteley will appreciate the full meaning of the joke.

London is great. You who have been there will know that it cannot be described in any one volume. Its past and present history is well worth reading, not only as entertaining, but as adding to one's stock of knowledge. Says Dr. Johnson: "Sir, the happiness of London is not to be conceived but by those who have been in it. I will venture to say there is more learning and science within the circumference of ten miles from where we sit, than in all the rest of the kingdom." I could talk days, yes months over all we saw in even the little time we spent here. Come around after office hours, I will fill the old Chesire mug and spin yarns till you are sleepy. Perhaps you are so now.

Letters of introduction had been given us to distinguished people residing near London, but we were unable to accept the invitations to call and dine, as the day following our arrival we were much indisposed from digestive trouble, no doubt caused by the water, and to cap the climax, a boil began in the inside of my nose. My feelings and appearance were a valid excuse for declining all social functions, so we stuck to the hotel and to the city till August 12th, at 12:30 P. M., when we left The London and North Western R. R. Station for Liverpool on our way home.

CHAPTER XXIV.

HOMEWARD BOUND.

"Home, there is a magic in that little word."

WE reached Liverpool at 4:30 P. M. The train was a "Special White Star Express," running in connnection with the ships of that Company. We rode through a beautiful country at a rapid rate, with but little motion to the cars, and everything about them more American than I had seen in Europe. The steamer "Majestic" was at the wharf. At 5 P. M. the plank was hauled in, and we began our second voyage over the Atlantic. We saw nothing of Liverpool, beyond a glimpse. There is an elevated railroad in the town, and what I could see of the docks and wharves during the short time between the arrival of the train, and the departing of the ship, merited all the praise I had heard concerning them. The train in which we ran over, was loaded with the most motley lot of baggage I ever saw. Trunks, bags, boxes big and little, things that should have gone by freight the day before. They all got there, however.

We reached Queenstown the next morning about 6 o'clock. For some cause the mails from

London were delayed, and we did not leave the harbor until 1:10 P. M. Many of the passengers went ashore, and had I known we should have been delayed so long, would have gone into the city and taken a ride in a jaunting car, with a pretty Irish maid. I do not know what Mary might have done. "The Emerald Isle" looks its color. While waiting, we were surrounded by bumboat women endeavoring to sell their wares, mostly alleged Irish laces in the shape of shawls, small blankets, hoods, and other ornamentations for the female form. I bought a few trinkets made from bog-wood.

When I went aboard the ship at Liverpool, I at once searched out the captain, (E. J. Smith, R. N. R.) to find if my clothing and rugs shipped from Genoa had been received. He said he did not know, but told me to ask the Second Steward. I asked him where I might find him, and again he said he did not know. If this was not ignorance, what is? It seemed to me a captain of so large a ship as the "Majestic" should know where a little thing like the Second Steward could be found. The package came to our room all right, soon after we got under way. At Queenstown a number of emigrants got on, three or four hundred at least. I remember one poor fellow who had brought his sister, or sweetheart, over on a tug. He was weeping bitterly, which rather makes me think it was a sweetheart. What a mystery lay before each. When will they meet again?

The mails put on were enormous. Bag after bag, directed to all parts of the world, China, Japan, Sandwich Islands, to South America, and to every State in our Union. It was several hours before they were stowed away in the hold. Time is taken from "Daunts Rock," just at the entrance to the harbor. On this trip the vessel made her best record, 5 days, 17 hours, 56 minutes to Sandy Hook Light Ship, beating all previous runs by 8 minutes. She had just come off the dock, after having new screws put in. The weather throughout the voyage was fine, a smooth sea, with now and then a fog. Fogs are terrors. Nothing I know but fire, is so much to be dreaded. Vastly denser than on land, you run into them in an instant, and after sailing on and on, the deep toned whistle blowing every sixty seconds, you run out as suddenly into the clear sunshine. On the banks of Newfoundland we encountered them most frequently. Here we saw many fishing smacks, which had come from the shores of France. At times when the fog lifted, we could see them not more than two or three ships lengths off the side. I have often wondered if many were not run down. I think it must be so, as it always appeared we ran faster at such times, for in speed, I should judge lay the element of safety. The faster you go the worse for the boat struck. The ship (Majestic) was an immense one, fitted up like a grand hotel, with every comfort a passenger could desire; good food, comfortable rooms, attentive service, but more than all else was a feeling of perfect safety, which added a charm to the voyage. These with judicious speed seem to be the aim of this line. I met several acquaintances, and two or three old hospital chums, and with them, revived old times in the smoke room. One fellow was thankful I was aboard, I feel sure. He was a Spaniard. One day he stood looking at the chart, while I was in the same state of action, when I spoke to him, making some comments on the run, he replied in such a way, I at once knew he did not understand me, and from his utterance was sure of his nationality, I opened wide in the best Spanish I could muster. That fellow never let go of me till I walked off the gang plank at New York. He told me he was almost dead for a talk, but could not buy it on board. The longer I live, the more fortunate I find it for the world at large I was born.

We did not bother about seats at table, taking what was left over. I went down into the saloon as soon as I could after leaving Liverpool to choose them, but found so long a line in waiting, I gave up the job as a bad one, preferring to be on deck, drinking in the ozone from the sea. We nevertheless got very good ones, with a very attentive waiter. This brings to mind the only example in the history of the world of not being able to fee an attache. It was at Naples, I think.

After paying everybody I could find, I went in search of "Boots". I found him asleep. I shook him, holloed at him, but could not awaken him, so left in disgust. I guess he had been out with the boys the night before. He'll have a monument one of these days.

Mary began "regulating" as soon as we were on board. We missed the genial good-fellowship of the "Lunatic," the doctor, the professor and his sister, as well as others who had been companions on the outward voyage. Consequently the passage was less lively and *we* did not run the boat as we had on the outward journey. To make up for this disappointment, we had compent officers, all members of the Royal Naval Reserve, a clean ship and a feeling should accident occur we should be well taken care of, as the discipline of the crew was perfect. If ever you go to Queenstown, or Liverpool, go by one of the "White Star" vessels. You'll get there if seamenship can accomplish it. We made up our minds it was a good time to talk over the events of the past three months, and enjoy each other's society. It was rather novel as there were not so many opportunities for "dont's" and anticipation rather than moral retrospection held the higher cards. Mary read a great deal. She found her favorite books in the library, "The Outlaws of Missouri" and "How to Win at Cards." Again we were unfashionable in not being ill, but eating all they gave us, with luncheons between. Our chairs were well situated, as I feed the deck steward to place them and keep us out of the sun.

We reached Quarantine about 3 A. M. Both of us felt so delighted we were soon to see our children and our home, we could not sleep, so got up and went on deck. It was a beautiful morning, cool and refreshing. We remained above till we landed. We saw the face of our son-in-law beaming at us from the wharf. We were told it was the intention of my daughter and son to meet us, but the ship arrived sooner than expected. We were just as glad to see him, if he was only a fraction of the family. The Custom House at New York is the worst in the world. They had the pleasure of pulling our trunks and bags inside out, and received their labors for their pains, as they found nothing dutiable under the then existting law. Mary is a first-class smuggler. Her garments presented a much different appearance when she reached home, than when the officer interviewed them. Then they were decked off in laces from Venice, Brussels, and Paris. Jewelry adorned her person and that bonnet. She was gorgeous. An hour after reaching the house of our daughter, they were the same old traps I had seen so often in our little journey in the world.

We remained a day in the city, and then returned to our nest, reaching our own fireside in just three months and two hours after leaving it.

On the ride up we had a chance to compare the virtues of American and Foreign cars. The palace car in which we were, seemed stuffy. A woman in the chair in front persisted in pulling down my shade, when I desired to look out. She wanted to run my seat as well as her own. The smoking compartment was filled with non-smokers, reading papers. I got a stool from the porter and sat in the vestibule. No such actions on the trains in Europe. Mary has her opinion, I have mine, we agree to disagree.

At the home station our daughter-in-law with many friends awaited our arrival. I shook hands with all the males, and kissed all the girls. I knew it was a last opportunity for a while. Our home had been decked with garlands of flowers by loving hands, prompted by loving hearts. Upon the waiter in the hall were cards innumerable congratulating us on our safe return. Friends began calling at once, so did practice. I had not been in the house an hour, before a patient, who had been suffering for some days, came for the performance of a minor surgical operation. As I had my instruments taken to my residence previous to my departure, I was armed, and speedily relieved him. We retired late.

The following morning I went to "Recovery Hall," and it seemed a long but pleasing journey, as I was so frequently stopped by friends who said they were glad to see me back. I found everything in good shape, and calls already upon the slate, all to "come at once." The old round of life's tread-mill began. I gave away the holy beads and the relics I had bought. I still regretted not having that toe-joint, yet it may be best that what is left of the poor Saint should rest in what is regarded by some as Holy Ground.

The Reporter of one of our prominent daily papers came to me after a few days, asking an interview, that the general public might know something of our trip in which it seemed to take much interest. I gave him a couple of columns. Since that time so many have heard me talk, have seen my enthusiasm, and asked so many questions, I decided to write down during my hours of idleness, something of our outing. I did not care for myself, I wished all to know about Mary. Sometimes I start talking of the many happy hours spent in Europe, growing more and more enthusiastic, when a gentle "don't" rings its familiar chestnut bell in my ears, and I cease.

Perhaps you wish to hear its music now. Pardon me, I am almost run down. I want to moralize a little, and as the sun comes in at my window this bright Sunday afternoon, like an old man I am tempted to grow garrulous. As I look back upon the days of which I have written, at best a brief and imperfect sketch, I think after all life is but a journey, the varying conditions into which we happen to fall being the different countries visited. In some we build palaces, in others we find ruins, it rests with us individually which it shall be. The higher and more complete the education, the more it seems to me a man is lifted up, the broader his thought, the freer his will. I have much to acquire, but I would not give back to that oblivion in which I once was, all I learned in this little journey, for many days of longer life, or a thousand times its cost. Travel in foreign lands teaches much of the history of one's own nation not learned in books. We see the progress of our race as it is going on, learning by comparison how man has come up from the lower to the higher; we see the Creeds of Christendom attired in their various garbs; we view the progress of principalities and powers, comparing Liberty with the rule of Monarchs; we gleam from the rich harvest, everywhere strewn about the lands through which we pass, that "ours" is not altogether the best, for we find among the other grains some fruitage better than we gather ourselves; we learn too by association with different peoples that life is given us, not for the selfish purpose of our own enjoyment, or reward here, or hereafter, but to make others happier, and that there is a recompense on this earth, if no other is expected elsewhere.

From all we have seen, from the cup of enjoyment from which we have drunk, we cannot help wishing all might taste the same luscious fruit we have eaten. It would correct the mental astigmatism, we know some of you have, and focus the beams of a brighter light upon your heart, if not upon your brain.

A great part of my enjoyment was due to Mary, my wife. Always the Safety-Valve on the Boiler of my Enthusiasm, she added what would otherwise have been wanting, and to her I owe much, Semper fides et fidelis. But I hear her calling, and as I have learned to obey, as well as to honor and to love, I must hasten to her.

To the countries we have visited, to the pleasures we have enjoyed, and to the reader who has followed our "sandal-shoon and scollop shell," we say—

AUF WIEDERSEHEN.

PRESS OF
WEBB & WINSLOW,
HUDSON, N. Y.

Brown Brothers & Co.,

59 Wall St., New York.

PHILADELPHIA--BOSTON.

ALEX. BROWN & SONS, BALTIMORE,

ALL CONNECTED BY PRIVATE WIRE.

Travelers' Letters of Credit.

**BILLS OF EXCHANGE.   CHEQUES.   .
TELEGRAPHIC TRANSFERS OF MONEY
TO ALL POINTS.   COLLECTIONS MADE
ON ANY PART OF THE WORLD.   .   .**

INVESTMENT : SECURITIES : A : SPECIALTY.

Brown, Shipley & Co.,

LONDON.

..WHITE STAR LINE..

UNITED STATES AND ROYAL MAIL STEAMERS,
New York, Queenstown and Liverpool.

MAJESTIC, 9965 Tons.   TEUTONIC, 9984 Tons.
GERMANIC, 5065 Tons.   BRITANNIC, 5004 Tons.
CYMRIC, 12,552 Tons.   ADRIATIC, 3887 Tons.

One of the above steamers sails from LIVERPOOL and NEW YORK regularly every WEDNESDAY, calling at QUEENSTOWN to receive and land mails and passengers.

The **"Majestic"** and **"Teutonic"** are twin-screw steamers, well know for their unsurpassed accommodations for all classes of passengers. The **"Cymric,"** a new twin-screw steamer 600 feet long and 64 feet beam, has very superior accomodations on upper decks for a limited number of saloon passengers. Owing to her great size, the accommodations for Third-class Passengers are exceptionally fine, including a large smoking room for men and a sitting-room for women. Also ample table room at meals. **"OCEANIC,"** now building at Belfast, will be 704 feet long and about 17,000 tons, the largest steamer ever built.

For rates, dates of sailing, Saloon or Second Cabin plans, apply at the office of the Company, 7 and 9 BROADWAY, BOWLING GREEN BUILDING, or to any of the Company's Agts.

❧COMPANY'S OFFICES❧

115 State Street, Boston.
406 Walnut St., Philadelphia.
133 E. Baltimore Street, Baltimore.
432 St. Paul St., Montreal.

244 South Clark Street, Chicago.
Cor. 9th and Olive Sts., St. Louis.
121 So. Third St., Minneapolis.
8 King Street, East, Toronto.

..The Raleigh..

Pennsylvania Ave., cor. 12th St.,

WASHINGTON, D. C.

 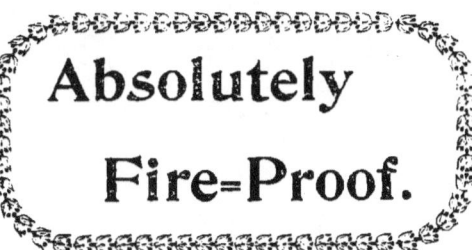

| Opposite New City Post Office...... | ACCESSIBLE TO ALL POINTS OF INTEREST IN THE CITY..... |

T. J. TALTY, Manager.

www.ingramcontent.com/pod-product-compliance
Lightning Source LLC
Chambersburg PA
CBHW020810230426
43666CB00007B/937